What People Are Sa
Why Have You Abandoned Me?

"*Why Have You Abandoned Me?* is like a mirror. The reader will be amazed to see himself or herself so clearly in the pages. The author helps us to move forward, unafraid, as we discover and learn the origins of our sensitive self which is easily hurt by being ignored or rejected. By recognizing failures or weaknesses of our upbringing, we can begin to understand how we are affected behaviorally and emotionally."

—Ernie Anastos, TV anchor, FOX News, New York

"*Why Have You Abandoned Me?* is a book written by a seasoned therapist who addresses one of the most powerful influences in our lives: parents. With gentleness and wisdom, Dr. Kalellis clarifies how we have been programmed in positive or negative way by close or distant parental influence and helps us to provide emotional and spiritual healing."

—Maria Sikoutris Di Iorio, MA, Ed.S.,
LPC Director of The Hellenic Therapy Center

"No matter how old you are, your relationship with your parents or parental adults—whether it was wonderful or painful—has had an impact on the person you are today. *Why Have You Abandoned Me?* is one of those rare books with the power to re-examine and recreate your emotional life, presenting insightful and spiritual options—one that can comfortably change you life for the better."

—Demetria De Lia, Ph.D.
Academy of Clinical and Applied Psychoanalysis

WHY
HAVE YOU
ABANDONED
ME?

Discovering God's Presence
When a Father Is Absent

A Crossroad Book
The Crossroad Publishing Company
New York

The Crossroad Publishing Company
www.CrossroadPublishing.com
© 2011 by Peter M. Kalellis

In continuation of our 200-year tradition of independent publishing, The Crossroad Publishing Company proudly offers a variety of books with strong, original voices and diverse perspectives. The viewpoints expressed in our books are not necessarily those of The Crossroad Publishing Company, any of its imprints or of its employees. No claims are made or responsibility assumed for any health or other benefit.

Printed in the United States of America.
The text of this book is set in [Apollo & Garamond]

Project Management by
The Crossroad Publishing Company
John Jones

For this edition numerous people have shared their talents and ideas, and we gratefully acknowledge Peter Kalellis, who has been most gracious during the course of our cooperation. We thank especially:

Cover design: Archer Graphics
Text design: Web Fusion
Acquisition and development: Gwendolin Herder

Message development, text development, package, and market positioning by
The Crossroad Publishing Company

Cataloging-in-Publication Data is available from the Library of Congress

Books published by The Crossroad Publishing Company may be purchased at special quantity discount rates for classes and institutional use. For information, please e-mail info@CrossroadPublishing.com.

ISBN 13:978-0-8245-2628-3
15 14 13 12 11

Table of Contents

Note on Scripture Citations

Throughout this book, the author quotes from various versions of the Bible. Unless set in quotation marks, the quotations should be understood as references that sometimes include the author's own translation or interpretation. Chapter and verse citations are provided for readers who wish to explore the scriptures further.

Acknowledgments

Why Have You Abandoned Me? Discovering God's Presence When a Father Is Absent owes its final form and completion to John Jones, the editorial director of The Crossroad Publishing Company. Diligently, John went over my manuscript and made certain valuable suggestions which made this book most inspirational reading.

I am grateful to—

- Gwendolin Herder, President of The Crossroad Publishing Co., who has encouraged my writing ambition and has been a proponent of my message for many years. Prior to this publication, Gwendolin has published three other books that I have written.
- The editorial department of The Crossroad Publishing Co. for comments and text improvements that made this effort worthwhile.
- Pat, my loving and nurturing wife who made sure to bring me a cup of tea and a cookie while I agonized for many hours at the computer to write this book.
- Margery Hueston and Pattie Manzi who diligently edited my last draft before I submitted it to the publisher.
- My loving children—Mercene, Michael, Basil, and Katina—and four grandchildren—Nikki, Andrew, Stacey-Mercene, and Peter-Andrea—who have taught me what love means and whose presence in my life has been a real inspiration.

Dedication

I dedicate this book to people of
all ages who sometime in their life
have felt ignored, rejected, or abandoned.

Prologue

The purpose of this prologue is to introduce the theme of this book—feelings of abandonment that result in loneliness. My fervent hope is to provide answers and healthy coping skills to combat those feelings and regain inner peace. The title, **Why Have You Abandoned Me?**, is a paraphrase of the words that Jesus uttered as He felt the agony of the cross: *My God, my God, why have You forsaken me?*

Jesus never felt alone. *My Father and I are one* is an affirmation of the intimacy that existed between Father and Son. Yet the Father disappeared; He was inexplicably absent. Where was the loving Father about whom Jesus had often spoken? Where was He at the critical time in His Son's life? Why didn't the Father help Him or give a sign of His presence during the tragedy of the Cross? In His human nature, Jesus felt abandoned and lonely. Hanging naked on the cross, mocked by the crucifiers, and breathing His last breath, He cried, "My God, my God, why have You forsaken me?" *Where are you? Why are you not helping me?*

Father, where were you when I needed you most? is the cry of every child who feels abandoned. It is the cry of every teenager in need of guidance while undergoing the confusion of physical and emotional development. To those of us who, for whatever reasons, missed our father or mother's presence, the cry continues to follow us into our adult years. Abandonment and the impending fear of emotional or physical death cause profound pain to most people who experience the absence of a father or fathering person to support, help, advise, and love them. The father's presence is needed to give reassurance even when a loving mother is present. As we grow up we learn from both the father and mother what it means to be a man or a woman. Through our adult years, the father's influence, positive or negative, remains present and is expressed as we interact with other people.

Most of us have *unfinished business* with our fathers that affects our relationships with spouses, children, friends, and associates at work, often causing profound feelings of loneliness, vulnerability, and anger. Even Jesus felt lonely and abandoned by his father.

※ ※ ※

This book is not about the death of Jesus Christ on the cross or about the purpose of His suffering and His feeling of forsakenness. It is not about the theology of redemption. It is, rather, an effort to provide comfort and healing to millions of wounded souls who continue to feel abandoned or neglected by their fathers or mothers who were emotionally or physically absent. Many of us who have bravely repressed the feeling of abandonment live a mediocre or miserable life, placing blame on current circumstances and sensing that something is missing. This missing part in our lives could be the absence of a father or mother. While most people know the importance of a mother's care and the importance of her loving presence in the development of a healthy child, contemporary psychology and research indicate major concerns about the equally important role of the father, and what happens when that role is interrupted for some reason (absent father syndrome).

If you are a father, a son or a daughter, a wife, or a mother who, at one time, has felt abandoned, abused, or neglected by your father, this book is for you. As you read each chapter, you will feel enriched, and gradually you will realize that your life has been continuously protected by the one and only Father who loves you unconditionally. Regardless of your present emotional or physical condition, your Heavenly Father is present. As you trust His caring presence in your life, comfort and confidence come from the holy scripture that promises *that all things work together for good for those who love God* (Rom 8:28).

The promise of the Father who accepts us and loves us unconditionally is vividly evident in the Gospel story of the Prodigal Son (Luke 15:11–32), a story we will turn to repeatedly in this book. The abandoned father joyfully reunites with his son and makes preparation for a great feast to celebrate the return of the boy who wasted his fortune on loose living. The father calls to the servants, "Quickly, bring out a robe—the best one—and put it on him; put a ring on his finger and sandals on his feet. Kill the fatted calf, and let us eat and celebrate, for this son of mine was dead and is alive again; he was lost and is found." And they celebrated the return of the Prodigal Son.

—PMK

1

The Problem Starts Early

All humans have their dark side, just as they have inner virtues. We are endowed with tremendous powers of resilience, and we owe it to ourselves and to our world to claim them. We can do many good things with our virtues when we are aware of our dark side.

Sensitivity to being abandoned, ignored, or rejected is part of the human condition. All human beings at some point in their lives go through a feeling of abandonment. The fear of abandonment starts at birth with everyone. After nine months of room service in the mother's womb, the infant emerges into a new environment feeling cold, hungry, and helpless. A loud wail marks the entry of air into the lungs; the infant has to breathe for itself. This is a remarkable moment. From the very beginning, this child experiences the awesomeness of life and the struggle for survival and wellbeing. Those who assist with or witness the birthing of a child wonder what the future holds for this tiny creature. The child appears puny and helpless—of all the creatures born into this world, it is among the most helpless and requires total care for a long time. Without being asked, the child is committed to the life that lies ahead.

Although the neonate is relatively complete, it can only survive with the aid of a helper. There is an inborn directedness for further growth and the potential for the very special type of adaptation that human beings require. At birth, infants possess a genetically determined biological endowment that is both common to all humankind and unique. Humans have a second heritage that they acquire after birth from those with whom they live. It is a heritage that has evolved over countless generations, one that children gradually refine and use for their own development.

Initially an infant's reality is physical, and its body needs nourishment, warmth, and cleanliness. It is totally dependent on its mother; it experiences loneliness when she is absent, and discomfort, hunger, and frustration when deprived of instant gratification. Mother, the designated nurturer, provides for all these needs. If these needs are not met, the child senses fear. If the mother does her job in a warm and dependable way, the child's natural anxieties develop in a moderate way, and the child is able to feel a sense of security.

A mother's contribution to the welfare and development of a child is important, but the continuation of mothering into a child's adult years can be destructive. Mother and child may cherish their interaction in later years, but as time evolves, a triangulation is being formed—father, mother, and child—which often causes dysfunction in the family life. Subconscious needs may turn the male child into a surrogate husband and the female child into a surrogate wife. At times, with tragic results, this can become incest; or the male, who has had no father to bond with, may transfer this need for a father figure to the mother, resulting in an Oedipal kind of relationship with mother. The child may interpret the father's absence as evidence of his own unworthiness. Feeling abandoned by his father, such a male has a hard time separating from the mother and has enormous difficulty in connecting with the real world.

Four of my current male clients, who are highly educated people holding good positions in society, are still living at home with their mothers. Unable to establish a relationship with a woman, they are busy taking care of their widowed or divorced mother, traveling with her, vacationing with her, and seemingly having a good time. It *seems* a workable system to those who know them. My question is: *Why are they so unhappy?*

Most therapists are aware of the abandonment issues that male and female clients experience, and the destructive issues that follow: inability to find fulfillment among colleagues, insecurity about their position in society, and inadequate partners in marriage.

In situations where there is no father present, a growing young man may gain comfort and guidance from a loving uncle, a caring mentor, or a spiritual father figure. The young person may look for a man he admires to provide a model that is not threatening to his independence, someone whose mentoring or guidance is comfortable. If he finds such a role model, he can be grateful for growing in a healthy manner and under God's abundant grace.

Adolescence is a period of great change in personality. It is a time of trial and initiation into manhood and womanhood. It is a time when a sense of one's self is forming, a sense that will last a lifetime. The cocoon of home safety breaks open and a butterfly emerges to discover the flowers in the garden. Out of the limbo world of adolescence, a man emerges. Many men do not feel adequately initiated into manhood and never do feel in full possession of their masculinity. They feel passive when they need to be assertive. They are unable to say with certainty what they want out of life. They make choices and then second-guess themselves. They oscillate between weakness and macho brutality. They feel a lack of masculinity, and they are afraid to pursue the love of a woman. In some cases, they disguise their insecurities with sweet talk or grandiose ideas.

It does not take long, however, before smart women discover their phoniness and drop them. In many instances, these problems in adulthood stem directly from the absence of a strong, positive male role model during formative years.

In his quest for manhood, a young person receives little help from other men who compete with him. Even when a father is present, a young man cannot accept much help from him because he, too, is trying to establish his identity separate from his family of origin. (As a modern form of initiation into manhood, having a mentor or finding sound and sensible psychotherapy may work for the growing adolescent who is open to it.)

Adolescents who are introverts need more time alone to process their experiences, and they become exhausted if forced to continually relate to others. They experience extroverts as loud and pushy. Introverts tend to be on the shy side and wait for the world to affect them. Extroverts, on the other hand, may see introverts as morose and passive. Extroverts rarely tire of being with people; they meet people easily and feel energized by them. The point is that whether an introvert or an extrovert, an adolescent, who is trying psychologically to develop into a man, needs something initiatory, a vehicle to take him into the adult world. It is important for him to see and find a model in a culture that does not automatically offer one to him.

Feeling unloved or abandoned by a parent always leaves scars, but the wound can be healed and healthy growth can begin anew. The challenge is to give up notions of having been abandoned. You are not a victim. Many young men of yesterday were subject to a culture that victimized them with shame, guilt, and worthlessness. It was always the victim's fate to suffer. A Greek song that was popular when I was in my early teens comes to mind:

As an orphan at a young age, I never smiled.
  No mother or father to love me and make me
    laugh.
When I see parents loving their children,
  My heart aches, my eyes brim with tears.
Whoever grows without a caring parent
  Becomes a victim in an unloving world,
Floating directionless and hopeless. What a sin!
  A rudderless boat abandoned in a stormy sea.

Young and abandoned children sang this song with passion. More than fifty years ago, I also sang that song, thinking of it as Biblical truth. Feeling the loss of my mother and missing my father who was working far away in a foreign land, I felt that the song was written for me. Perhaps it helped me and all those who sang it to survive parental absence and lack of love. Lucky are those who are able to leave victim mentality behind; there are better ways to feel okay. Personally, I did leave behind the *poor me* attitude—*little Peter the orphan,* as perceived by my relatives. Wallowing in self-pity serves no purpose. It takes an effort, however, to exchange victimization for authentic movement and acceptance of reality.

Lack of love or abandonment of a child does not mean that the child is not worth loving. Parental physical absence or emotional unavailability is never a child's fault, and the child should not feel that it is his or her fault. With the exception of death and the possibility of a wounded father or mother, the issue is often parental lack of awareness—ignorance of parenting. Of course we cannot totally blame a father or a mother for their lack of parenting skills. Some parents probably grew up without parental support themselves; they were abandoned and unloved.

If we assume that most of us have experienced or may have to face abandonment at some time in our lives, we need to learn how to use healthy defense mechanisms to protect ourselves from anger or isolation. Some people are able to avoid the pain of abandonment through isolation. They build walls around themselves to avoid the trauma and hurt. A man in his mid-forties told me that he has no contact and does not want to have contact with his parents. He blocked out whatever good they had done for him. "They never did anything for me," he said. Obviously, he had numbed himself. "I like my life as it is. I'm fine," he said, trying to convince himself that he was safe from hurt. Beyond any doubt, people who deny or repress their feelings cannot relate honestly with others. Unfortunately, an *I-don't-care* attitude surfaces in intimate relationships, especially in marriage.

When an emotionally abandoned person starving for acceptance and love enters a relationship, the partner may have a hard time responding to such a needy person. If the abandoned person's need for affection, attention, and acceptance is constant, the other person eventually feels burdened and may run away. If both people in an intimate relationship have similar needs, their expectations continually rise, and the result is frustration, disappointment, or anger. Here is another phenomenon familiar to family therapists: An abandoned or rejected person finds a loving partner who is able to provide love and acceptance. Initially, the interaction is pleasant for both. As the relationship develops and seems promising to both, the abandoned person behaves in a way that disappoints or even hurts the loving partner. Unconscious mechanisms are at work, forcing the abandoned person to repeat his or her experience with abandonment, *a covert sabotage*. Abandoned people relive their old familiar patterns. Why? The only comforting answer for me is that in reliving past pain, their soul searches for healing, which is only available when they turn to the ultimate healer, God, in faith, prayer, and good behavior.

If you are facing abandonment or rejection by a significant person in your life, how can you lessen your emotional pain? It would be a mistake to repress it and pretend it was not there. The truth is that repression of feelings influences much of our behavior. Repression is a subtle form of denial to protect us from facing a painful truth. Regardless of how deeply we bury our hurt feelings, some day they surface and stifle a mature attitude towards the realities of life. Repression can become depression if we are unable to register the feelings when they occur.

There are other methods of dealing with feelings of abandonment. One damaging defense mechanism is rationalization. Some people find reasons to justify or explain the fact that they felt neglected or rejected or abandoned by those whose love, nurture, and support they needed. Others revert to patterns that actually belong to childhood, instead of operating on an adult level. Sometimes adults with a child's mentality move away from home and gain some independence. Initially it feels good! Yet if for any reason they are forced to move back home, they find the parents who once rejected them to be more loving and accepting. As a result, they are caught in a conflict. While they value the feeling of independence away from home, they also enjoy the acceptance, nurturing, and love they receive at home. So they decide to stay at home. As a result, they prevent themselves from assuming adult roles. Feeling needed, they say such things as *It's time for me to do something for my Mom and Dad. Poor Dad had to work three jobs to support our family. We hardly saw him. We wanted him to talk to us. It seemed impossible for him to spend time with me or my sister. Dad was a good provider, but not a good father. My Mom, being an only daughter, had to take care of her sick parents every day. She also worked as a waitress at night to supplement the family income. When she came home, she was so tired that she could hardly speak to me, but I know she loved me.*

Certain people, however, deal with abandonment or rejection out of either guilt or gratitude with what seems to be a positive approach. They reach out to parents with overwhelming love. They feel the need to repay their parents for all they did for them. Others feel subtle resentment for having to put their lives on hold and care for their parents, but they compromise. In being good to their parents, they are rewarded with the valuable gift of parental approval.

Thoughts You May Consider

- Most people are sensitive to the fear of abandonment. Each one of us needs to understand and deal with this feeling realistically. That is, we cannot expect to be accepted, loved, or understood by everyone. People deal with their own adverse circumstances and challenges. We can be content if there is at least one person in our life who meets our needs. In that case, we need to show reciprocity.

- Total acceptance and unconditional love come to us only from a unique source, God the Giver of all the good and perfect gifts of life. Guidance and strength come from Christ. Even a glimpse into His Gospel offers explicit evidence of His compassion and love. Read the story of the Prodigal Son, or the Sinful

Woman who was sentenced to death by stoning. *Let the one without sin cast the first stone,* Jesus said, teaching us not to be eager to judge or to have an unforgiving heart.

- In the sight of God, we are His adopted daughters and sons. God asks us to refocus our attention, challenge our negative thoughts, re-examine how we respond to life, and correct our ways. Through St. Paul, we are reminded *to be anxious for nothing, but in everything by prayer, supplication, and thanksgiving let our requests be made known to God. And the peace of God, which surpasses all comprehension, shall guard our hearts and our minds in Christ Jesus.*

- If approval is important to us and we are trying under all circumstances to find it, let's try an experiment and stop looking for two weeks. Let us suppose we do not try to please everybody or have high expectations of others. Chances are that we may regain peace of mind and be less stressed. Our belief that we have already been approved by God and live under His grace suffices. We can reconsider His unconditional love for us and be ever grateful for His presence in our lives.

- Divorce or death of either mother or father can deprive us of parental approval and keep us in search of a benevolent being who will approve of us. As abstract as it may sound, we need to find an ideal father or mother image within ourselves. In essence, we need to be a benevolent parent to ourselves. The ultimate and most comforting resolution is to realize that we have a caring Heavenly Father, the kind of loving father that every father should be. Our belief in Him can give us deep, emotional satisfaction.

2

Abandonment: Its Effects?

We never dreamt that some bad things that have happened to us were ever going to happen. That is why we are so devastated when they do happen. We all want a reason for what happens to us. We want to know why, so that we can once again have a sense of order and predictability about life.

Have you ever been abandoned by a friend with whom you had shared good times and personal secrets? Have you ever been abandoned by someone with whom you were deeply in love and were planning to marry? Has either your father or your mother left the family nest due to death or divorce? If so, then you have an idea about the effects of abandonment. Basically, it is an emotional experience shared by many people who have been left behind by someone they loved and trusted. Abandonment causes emotional pain that differs from person to person. It generates sadness, self-doubt, insecurity, loneliness, and fear—sometimes the feelings become hard to define.

Abandonment is about loss of love itself, that crucial loss of connectedness. It represents a human fear we all experience, dating back to our lost childhood when we were helpless and dependent and feared the loss of a parent or caregiver. Even our adult functioning temporarily seems to collapse if some significant person abandons or rejects us. Abandonment often involves breakup or betrayal. People struggling with abandonment issues include not only those who were neglected as children, but also those who experience the ending of a relationship through divorce or death.

Abandonment creates a force within many people that keeps them from being authentic human beings. Some people are so driven by the need to be loved and accepted that they lose their own identity during the search for acceptance. They mimic the ways in which others act, dress, talk, think, believe, or function, in the hope of gaining love and acceptance. Unresolved abandonment issues can interfere with future relationships. Not being accepted or appreciated or loved by someone significant results in a feeling of rejection or depression—a sad situation.

As we sharpen our focus on the concept of abandonment, we realize that it is a feeling of isolation. The abandoned person feels alone—not by choice. In my practice I have often dealt with broken hearts resulting from the sudden end of long-term romantic relationships that had big promises and plans for a shared future. Whatever conflict occurs between lovers resulting in a breakup, one will feel abandoned. When a husband leaves his wife for another woman, the abandoned wife feels alone—certainly not by choice. When a woman leaves her fiancé for a more successful and wealthier man, the jilted lover feels alone—and not by choice. Children feel abandoned when a parent moves out of the house. A wife whose unique purpose in life is to be a devoted mother may feel abandoned once her children move out of the house to create their own lives, *although rationally, she fully understands that this is the natural course of life.*

Abandonment is all of this and more. Rejection, withdrawal of love, criticism, or desertion create devastating emotional injury. When we are ignored, we are often cut all the way to the core. We lose not only our loved one, but often our sense of self as well. Feelings of abandonment come from a wide range of experiences. A person who has lost his job, and with it his professional identity, financial security, and status, may experience abandonment and may feel worthless until another job is secured.

Angered, the victim of abandonment focuses on his or her victimizer, the abandoner. Abandoners come in every possible size, shape, shade, age, and disposition. The perceived abandoner could be a parent, a son or a daughter, a relative, a friend, or a boss. While I wrote this chapter, I was dealing with five clients who felt emotionally abandoned by significant others.

✳ ✳ ✳

For example, **Karen** attributes her current conflicts and inability to adjust to life to her mother. *Mom was a control freak—always telling me how to dress, how to style my hair, and who to choose as my friends. When a boy phoned me, she wanted to know who he was and what he wanted. After nine o'clock each evening she took my cell phone so I wasn't able to talk to anybody. Last month I became thirty years old, and I still don't have a boyfriend.* Karen perceived her mother as a person who did not care how her daughter felt. Emotionally abandoned, Karen moved out of the house and decided not to have much contact with her mother. In this case, the abandoned became an abandoner.

Andy's self-esteem suffered the final blow when he discovered his only friend was having an ongoing affair with his wife. *I never had many friends; I have been a homebody. But* *when I met Barry at work we hit it off great, and I thought of him as a soul mate. I loved him as a brother. He was a bachelor and I often invited him to my house for dinner, especially on holidays. Little did I know that he would one day stab me in the back. I don't trust anybody anymore.* Understandably, Andy abandoned his friend Barry, disconnected emotionally from his wife, and he himself feels abandoned.

Sandra hates her boss, a middle-aged man whom she used to admire. She runs his busy office. Her boss is a real estate lawyer who spends little time in his office. She feels abandoned. *He spends his brief time in the office talking on the phone,* said Sandra. *He piles work on my desk and expects me to finish it in an hour. "We have deadlines," he explains. I'm the only employee in the office, and I do so much work I haven't time for lunch, but he never shows any appreciation. To crown it all, he's stingy. When I asked him for a raise, he told me he hasn't made any profit lately.* Sandra did not feel appreciated; she felt abandoned when left alone to deal with mounds of office work.

It is often difficult to differentiate between those with whom it is safe to become attached and those with whom we might have problems—who is worthy of trust, and who is an abandoner. Instead of investing time and precious energy dealing with an abandoner, we can be in a better state of mind if we try to apply tools of recovery, starting with our own best qualities. Surprisingly, we may discover a wellspring of positive power within ourselves.

Theodore, a well-known pharmacist in his town, went into therapy three months ago. His wife, a social worker, left him for one of her colleagues. Ted, as he preferred to be called, asked her to join him in marriage counseling, but she was unyielding. Married to him for seven years, she felt trapped;

she wanted to move on with her career and she wanted to pursue a doctoral degree. Ted attended his therapy sessions faithfully. To supplement his knowledge in the field, he read every self-help book available and attended seminars on relationships. None of this, however, could eradicate his distress. One day he came to my office with a huge box. *I've brought you a present,* he said with a smile. *You may open it now if you like.* Curious, I opened the box. It was neatly packed with the latest self-help books on the market. *You may have these,* he said. *I've read all of them, but I still feel unsettled. Nobody really cares how I feel.* He felt emotionally abandoned.

✳ ✳ ✳

Mental disturbance and behavioral dysfunction caused by unresolved abandonment have destructive consequences. Abandonment becomes the source of anxiety, insecurity, addictions, compulsions, stress, and other self-defeating behaviors. Abandoned people resort to eating excessive amounts of food, using alcohol and drugs, gambling, and getting into debt. Abandoned people are unable to connect with others and establish relationships. They feel unloved and have a hard time loving. Abandoned people feel inadequate when they are asked to perform a job. Unable to let go and move forward, they often feel stuck in a job they hate. Beyond the insight offered in self-help books, such as "Find happiness from within," abandoned people need to take action. If you are stuck in life, feeling unhappy, isolated, overly sensitive, suspicious, or depressed, there is hope in the healing power of Jesus Christ. Turn to Him for solace and direction.

Often when clients come to my office seeking help for their depression and despondency, I ask them to tell me what past painful events or sadness they are keeping alive in the present. Their answers are similar, expressing a cry for love. As children, some of them felt abandoned by a parent because of real or perceived parental neglect, anger, or rage. Others tell me that their parents divorced; they remember quarrels and felt no love. It is difficult to feel accepted in the world if we have never felt at peace in our own home. The feeling of abandonment in early childhood remains with us into adulthood; it is a handicap that is hard to shake off.

This feeling of not belonging has been my own nemesis for most of my life. In my training to become a psychologist and in my personal pursuit of a spiritual identity, I gradually realized the origins of this abandonment feeling and how it handicapped my progress through life. It started when I was two and a half years old; that was when my mother died. My father returned to his homeland, Greece. Six months later, he remarried and I found myself in a family that consisted of myself, my stepmother, and my father. During the following seventeen years in that house the nagging feeling of not belonging was ever with me. In school I had mixed feelings; sometimes I was accepted and sometimes not. I had three lasting friends with whom I played and shared. I felt that the rest of my schoolmates did not accept me. They called me *Americanaki*—little American—in a derogatory tone, and they did not want me in their company.

Obviously, early feelings are essential, for they work together to give us our sense of identity. I was fortunate to have a mentor, Father Papavasile, the priest of our little village who truly influenced my life. He taught me how to chant church hymns and in his own simple manner he made me realize that God is our heavenly Father—the kind of father a father should be—one who can give us unconditional love and deep emotional satisfaction. God not only accepts us but is pleased to call us His sons and daughters. That puts us in a secure position with Him in His family.

When I entered the adult world, eager to meet social standards and be accepted, emotional insecurities of early childhood pulled me away from God's family. I continued to attend church regularly and I believed in God, but my faith was anemic. *Continuing to play the role of an abandoned child carries a high price tag.* Like the Prodigal Son, my search for success and happiness interfered with my peace of mind. The feeling of not belonging resulted in inner misery, followed by an ulcer and major surgery.

During a long period of recovery from both physical and emotional setbacks, I had time to reminisce about my roots and my life in Moria, the Greek village where I grew up, with its simple folks who were happy with the little they had. I relived the melodic church services conducted by the humble servant of God, Papavasile, in whose presence people felt the presence of God. I had a vivid recollection of my school days. Every single day, I walked almost four miles to school and four miles back home, sometimes barefoot and lonely, always feeling the joy of passing by seven chapels and chanting hymns along the way. My comfort and my heritage!

As I compared the joy and simplicity of the village life with American affluence, I kept asking many questions. Why should Americans have such an abundance of everything? Instead of being grateful to live in America, I felt challenged. No material possessions or modern conveniences seemed to please me. Only gradually when I turned to God in fervent prayer did I find relief and peace—no rituals or formal services and pre-written prayers, but genuine connection with a *Father* who accepted me, a prodigal son. I rediscovered God in the personality of Jesus Christ, His Son, and spoke to Him as I would speak to a dear friend. It is only when I honestly and by faith speak to Jesus that I sense the potential in me that is able to make me whole. My reassurance comes from reading St. Paul's Epistle to the Colossians:

> *Strip off the old self with its practices and clothe yourselves with the new self, which is being renewed in knowledge according to the image of its Creator*

> (Col 3:9–10)

St. Paul's words had a tremendous effect on my mind. It was time for me to strip off my old self and clothe myself with the new self. A change was at hand. I needed a more positive attitude and more accurate thoughts of how I perceived myself and the world around me. Eventually, God found me in my state of avoidance in facing the reality of life. I replaced doubts with confidence in His love. Today His gift of grace that is a relentless pursuit motivated by love allows me to know and understand the truth about who I am. God's grace allows me to be me, to experience feelings of love, anger, anxiety, forgiveness, joy, and all emotions. Being loved and accepted unconditionally offers reassurance that I can decrease my weaknesses and increase my strengths. I can also decrease the gap between my inward and outward experiences in relationships. This newness of life surfaces in my interaction with my clients. With humility I connect with them without the distraction of intellect and process all their emotions, not as a psychologist but as a human being as I am now, stripped of preconceived notions and theories.

Thoughts You May Consider

- Whenever you find yourself in a state of abandonment by parents, relatives, or friends, avoid being a victim. In the eyes of God no one is abandoned. The evidence is very clear in the Gospel. Jesus never rejected or abandoned anyone. He accepted everyone with unconditional love.

- It is emotionally painful to feel abandoned. It may be helpful to examine yourself and see if you have done anything to justify that feeling. If you have, and you believe that the abandoner had a reason to reject you, take the first step. Go to him or to her and in a gentle spirit pursue reconciliation.

- If you are feeling emotionally abandoned, it is important for you not to wallow in self-pity or think of yourself as an ill-fated person. As a survivor you have already experienced the anguish of love-loss, yet you must have the courage to continue believing in people and in your own capacity to love. You may be faced with the struggle to remove obstacles in the way of finding a new kind of love.

- Sometimes an abandoned person becomes another person's loving and permanent partner; at other times, an abandoned person becomes an abandoner. If the person of your dreams has abandoned you, be careful not to become an abandoner yourself, either because of life's complex conditions or because of rage. Feeling bitter towards others may cause you to have a negative attitude towards people who could be loveable and loving.

- Fear of abandonment is the abdication of God's power within you. Be careful not to give power or control over your own life to others. What other people may think, feel, or say about you cannot and should not determine what you think and feel about yourself. Self-satisfaction is a result of being in charge of your life and believing in yourself. God has a purpose for your being in this world.

3

When Fathers Are Absent

Every human being is endowed with intelligence, will, memory, imagination, and sensitivity. These gifts of nature are mechanisms that enable energies, qualities, and dynamisms to flow forth from each person. In time of major adversity, these gifts provide healing and new direction.

Emotional depravation, conflicts, and complications arise and develop in the life of a child when the father is absent from the family unit because of either divorce or death. Regardless of how loving and sensitive a mother may be, the child still seeks the presence of the father to provide the male model that represents stability and strength. When there is divorce and the father is no longer present, the child's world changes. The home climate often becomes hostile, confusion sets in, and the child keeps asking, *Is Daddy coming back?* Although divorce is an adult issue, the child pays the price. Divorce affects the child's mind. Divorce is the death of a marriage, but it is not the death of a relationship. No matter how far apart from each other the parents may be, the relationship continues to live on, and the child's emotions are caught between the hammer and the anvil, causing insecurity. Children survive, oscillating between two parents and feeling confused. *Why do these two grown-ups, who at one time seemed to love each other, now want to live apart? How could they do such a thing to me? What's going to happen to me? I want both of my parents to be together with me.*

The Absent Father Syndrome encourages a mutually collusive *embrace*, with the mother nourishing a shared illusion of *oneness* from which the developing child cannot extricate himself, leaving him neither in nor out of the womb but wedged halfway between, half-alive, half-born. The mother sees her son with longing and admiration, as she initially saw her husband. The growing son absorbs his *mom's* affections, and he reciprocates with fervor to make her happy. He finds it hard to leave home. There's no woman like Mom.

The Physically Absent Father

I have a vivid recollection of fifteen-year-old Anthony playing basketball with adolescent enthusiasm. I was exhilarated by his strength and talent. I now see him again, about twenty years later, and he looks like a man of sixty. He walks with a perpetual slouch; he looks empty and vaguely guilty. He comes and goes according to his fixed routine, anchored, or more precisely, chained to his mother's apartment to which he returns from his routine job to eat his routine meals at the routine hour. When Anthony was seventeen, his father was killed in an automobile accident. Feeling protective and somewhat guilty about his young and still beautiful mother, Anthony was determined to become the man of the house. His mother, passive and self-indulgent, reinforced his assumed and distorted attitude about himself by making him the important man in her life. As invariably happens in such situations, what passed for filial dedication was, in fact, a forfeiture of a young man's potential. Relinquishing a large part of his own nature and attempting to carry the burden of a relationship to which he was not equal, the boy withered prematurely. Anthony's was an unfortunate story I have seen many times. Men like him sometimes remain single all of their lives. In some cases, when the mother dies the son soon marries. My own uncle married for the first time at the age of 65. With a smile, I asked him why he had waited so long. His answer came out slowly: "I could not get married as long as my mother was alive."

When a father dies, after a period of mourning and sadness, most children are able to see their father in their minds. They remember how it felt to sit on Dad's lap and smell his shaving lotion. They remember him doing difficult jobs; he rotated the tires of the family car, and in the fall, he climbed swiftly up a ladder to clean the gutters. Later in life, children remember the incidents vaguely, and details are forgotten. They feel sad and lonely and miss the presence of their father. An unvoiced cry lingers on: *Everybody else has a daddy except me.* They often become angry. In a situation of loss, anger is normal. *How could Daddy leave me if he really loved me? Didn't he care what might happen to me?* Feeling angry usually makes a child feel guilty. *I must be a terrible kid. How could I be angry with my Dad? I loved him very much, and I know he loved me.*

Sooner or later, these memories fade. Children grow and their lives change. They observe other children without a father. Eventually, a special "goodbye" is understood, a sort of *My Dad has died,* and children remember the feelings, rather than the face or smells or touches. They recall their father's hobbies or strengths, his way of playing or joking with them, his absence from home at night as they slept. Gradually the time comes when children realize that their father will never return. God's power within, that miracle of life, enables them to face the fact that they will never be with their father again. They become stronger. It is a great comfort when we realize how true is the statement of Christ: *The Kingdom of Heaven is within you* (Luke 17: 21).

God has placed within our soul all the ability we need to cope with any situation in our lifetimes. We have to believe in ourselves so that the existing strength that is present in our soul will be released. As we repeat Christ's statement, *The Kingdom of Heaven is within me,* we lack nothing. God's abundance, peace, power, and wisdom will be within us to face any challenges in life.

Stephen's Story

Stephen's father came back to his family from Iraq in May 2007. He was happy to be with his wife and son after two years in the desert. He felt lucky that he had survived several encounters with enemy forces. Once at home, he could not stop thinking about the thousands of lives that had been lost in Iraq. He kept telling stories to his family, and his mind still wondered, *Why war?* His son Stephen had grown as tall as his father. He was opinionated about American foreign policy. He spoke vehemently about the injustice of the war in Iraq and pointed out the ease with which the American government got involved in one war after another. His father noticed Stephen's assertive anti-war attitude and suggested that he was too young to understand politics and that his attention ought to be focused on schoolwork and his plans for college.

"College?" Stephen said vehemently. "Soon after high school, I'm going to Canada."

"Why Canada?"

"D'you think I'm gonna stay around here and be sent to Iraq?"

"The war will be over by the time you graduate."

"Sure, Dad. Then the U.S. will be involved in another war in another country," Stephen said with a smirk.

"How can you say that?"

"Let's face it, Dad—war makes America wealthy."

"You don't know what you're talking about," his father answered, annoyed.

Hearing the father-son debate, the mother stepped in to pacify both of them. "Daddy is home, and we ought to be happy. Tomorrow we are going to church to thank God," she said.

Stephen interrupted. "What are you going to say to God about Andy's dad who was killed in Iraq last year?"

Stephen's father was physically and emotionally absent and could not connect with his son. Later, his mother and father spent an entire evening discussing Stephen's situation.

"We must be patient with Stephen," said his mother. "He missed you terribly during the last two years, and now that you're back with us he's feeling sad for Andy. Our son loves you. He's confused."

"What am I supposed to do?"

"Love him," she said. "Show him that you're a good father who cares."

"He stays out late at night. I don't know who his friends are! I haven't seen him opening a book lately. Have you?"

"I hear the voice of an angry father. I know you love your son."

"I don't like the way he reacts to me."

A part of Stephen did resist his father's presence. Stephen was given a curfew. His father decided that he must be home by 10:00. Arguments and complaints became a daily issue. Tension and outbursts of anger stifled Stephen's vitality. Soon to be sixteen and having gone too far in defying his father, he suspected that he would not be allowed to go for his driving permit.

He wanted to act manly. He felt that something within was missing. In private, his mother advised him not to be so oppositional. "When your father went to war, you missed him and you were probably afraid he might be killed. But he's back. Like other soldiers, your father risked his life for a good reason: to protect the freedom of our country. Many fathers never came back. They are killed in war. Their children will miss them; they will never see their fathers again. We are lucky your father is back. It's time to help him understand that you're a growing young man and you're happy he's back safely."

"What can I say? When I say anything, he gets angry," Stephen said.

"Say nothing. Simply show respect and cooperation."

"Respect? When he's on my back?"

"Have you ever thought that he's trying to make you a strong man?"

"By trying to control me?"

"You need to reconcile with your father," she said. "Otherwise I won't cover up for you or do you favors anymore. Sometimes you are arrogant. If you want your father to be good to you, cooperate."

Stephen realized his mother had a point. He knew that a change of attitude was needed, but he wanted to prove that he'd done nothing wrong. Eventually he began to strive for a better relationship with his father. First, he apologized for talking back. As the climate at home improved, he became more available to help with chores. He washed the family car and even cleaned and painted his room. He had not understood why his father had to go and fight a war in a foreign land. He had felt abandoned. But things were finally beginning to stabilize.

A week before Christmas on an extremely cold day, Stephen polished his father's car until it looked like new.

"Is that my car? I can't believe it!" His father smiled at his son's effort to please him. "I might let you drive it some day. First, you need a driver's permit." Then he turned around, opened his wallet, and said, "You deserve a big tip."

Stephen gave his father a quick hug and ran to his friend's house.

The process of reconciling with his father did not take long. He had great support from his friend Andy, who appreciated Stephen's friendship. "You're lucky—your Dad came back," he said. These two boys played basketball together and had serious conversations about the current war. They shared their personal concerns. The parental influence was subtle and strong. Stephen's mother was patient and firm. Her parents had not been available to her; she had been raised by a grandmother who was a teacher. It was from her grandmother that she learned to love her church and read the Bible. She grew up to be a good storyteller, making even old stories come to life. When Stephen one evening angered his father by staying out after his curfew, his mother told him the story of the Prodigal Son. When the Prodigal Son had wasted his time and his wealth, he decided to return to his father and ask for forgiveness. His father received him back happily. He embraced him and kissed him and prepared a big celebration. Father and son reconciled.

"Mom, I know why you told me that story. But I'm not like the Prodigal Son."

"I know," she said, as a tear escaped her. She smiled and said, "But the angels in heaven rejoice when reconciliation and love prevail between father and son." It was her hope and prayer that Stephen and his father would love each other. A pillar of faith and love, she wanted harmony in her household.

"Your father is showing you what it means to be a man. Whatever you learn from your father you can amplify and improve on, on your own. Some day you'll be a better father to your children. This evening, when your father comes home, find a moment and give him a hug. Tell him you love him."

From that day, the topic of reconciliation with his father was in Stephen's mind. He knew what he had to do. His father had gone to war and come back alive and whole. Like a full-grown tree, his father, facing the challenges of his life, had taken his form and shape. Stephen too had to grow up. *A tree cannot grow under another tree.* He was still growing, and although he could not grow under his father, he had to adjust to his father's expectations and wishes as long as he was under his roof.

The Emotionally Absent Father

Some of my male clients give me the impression that they are emotionally wounded. They have a hard time fully accepting or appreciating their current life. In certain cases they are still suffering from the absence of their father in their early years. At times, the father was physically present but emotionally unavailable to both child and mother. We will call this experience the *absent father syndrome.* The question is: *Was the father excluded from family life, or did he exclude himself?* More likely than not, a combination of both factors was at work.

First, there is an unconscious collusion between mother and child to maintain and prolong their mutually inter-dependent omnipotence and dependency. They form a pair, a dyad, to satisfy one another's needs and wishes.

Second, closeness and involvement with the child, or distance and avoidance, may be the result of the father's unresolved psychological conflicts with his own father. These conflicts interfere with his role as a caring and loving father to his children.

The significance of the father in the formation of the child's personality is a major issue. Whether the infant is a boy or a girl, the father's emotional response to the infant and his attitudes toward the "mothering" are most significant. These observations substantiate a common reproach from clients who are only half alive emotionally: that their fathers did not support them in their attempts to develop their identity.

Fortunately, fathers in our times are increasingly involved in the upbringing of their offspring, especially when the wives have to return to work outside the home because of the increasing cost of living. According to the American Sociological Association the time fathers spend with their children has doubled over the past four decades. Across the country, fathers are more available to their families, provide more childcare, help more with schoolwork, and supervise more extracurricular activities. In some places the stereotype still persists that dads are not involved, but increasingly they are, and we should welcome this shift. The National Center for Education Statistics indicates that when fathers and mothers are both involved in their children's education, students tend to get better grades and enjoy school more.

As we rediscover the *emotionally absent father,* and pursue reconciliation, we facilitate healing for the wounded and emotionally deprived souls. Not too long ago I attended a funeral of a neighbor. At the cemetery after the burial, a young man stood alone under a tree a bit far from the graveside and stared at the sky. He was the son of the deceased. I knew him and went to him to offer my condolences.

"Thanks," he replied with an attempt at a smile.

"John, are you okay? I see you are deep in thought."

His teary eyes looked at me and he shook his head. "Not really." He paused for a few seconds and turned toward his father's newly dug grave. "I never heard the words '*I love you*' from my dad, and I'm sad that I never put my arms around him and said, '*I love you, Dad.*'" Conceivably, that memory will be in John's life for a long time before it eventually fades away, if ever. The hope is that some day when he becomes a father himself, he will be more sensitive to his children.

In most relationships, each member contributes some part to the emotional satisfaction or deterioration of the relationship system. The bittersweet comedy *Memories of Me* is a father-son movie. Billy Crystal as Dr. Abbie Polin is the son, and Alan King as Abe, a mediocre Hollywood actor, is the father. As I watched their verbal interaction, I was reminded that we cannot randomly blame the father for all the wrongs. Children play their part as well. In this movie, the son, an arrogant New York heart surgeon, is long estranged from his father. When the son suffers a mild heart attack, he makes an effort to connect with his father to repair the relationship, hoping in this way to bring equilibrium into his own life. This proves well-nigh impossible: the father, the self-described *King of the Hollywood Extras,* is not only a play-actor in Tinseltown but in life itself, refusing to take on any real responsibilities, least of all the responsibility of parenthood. With sarcasm and hostile remarks against his wife, he tries to justify his absence from his son's life. As far as Abe is concerned, his only *family* consists of his fellow extras. Though Abbie is extremely judgmental of his father, he himself is no prize in the commitment department, especially when dealing with his longtime lady friend who is hoping to marry him. The movie's final sequence is Abe's funeral.

This part of the movie brought back to my memory the picture of John standing alone under a tree after his father's funeral and thinking: *I'm sad that I never put my arms around him and said,' I love you, Dad.'* As a therapist, I suspected that this son, too, must have contributed something to his emotionally unavailable father.

It so happened that three months later, I received a phone call from John. He said he had problems and wanted to see me. He was in therapy because he suffered from a host of psychosomatic symptoms: acute attacks of anxiety, allergies, a sense of *not-enough-ness* escalating into spells of ambition and giddiness followed by withdrawal and unavailability to his friends. He claimed he had started to read the Bible daily, looking for answers. His involvement in a scholarly search of the scriptures drew my interest.

In his weekly therapy sessions he appeared motivated, revealing information that caused his distress, and after six months, he concluded he was cured and additional therapy was unnecessary. With regard to quick cures, I'm watchful because of the seductive sensations that accompany them; they can infect both therapist and client. I did not wish to be lulled into an artificial sense of achievement that would lead me to think, *What a great therapist I am! I can provide instant healing!*

John's intention to depart hastily was a warning signal that something alarming and painful was about to be uncovered. Defenses are questionable, and John's newly acquired but precarious equilibrium seemed to put him at risk. Flight from therapy was his only escape. His attempt to terminate therapy was based on the feeling of relief that he experienced—*no more anxiety, no more asthma, I'm feeling good*. Was there something else that seemed threatening to him or to our relationship?

Gently I said, "John, sometimes therapy, besides being expensive, tends to be tedious and emotionally taxing, but you have made some progress. Are you sure you want to quit now?"

"If something else comes up, I'll call you."

"Not a problem," I said.

He lingered for a few seconds, holding the doorknob and glancing at my diplomas on the wall. He slowly opened the door, and without looking at me, he said, "Why don't I come back just once more next week?"

Pandora's Box was opened at the next session. John angrily said, "I'm really a miserable fool who staggers and blunders about and doesn't want to face anything. I'm a pathetic poor little guy who can't attack and can't be attacked. I experience phases of nothingness. Life is frozen, sexless, and numb. I feel anonymous. Everything I've ever done was for someone else, to keep things just as they were. I've never done anything original in my life. My mother told me I was nearly suffocated at birth. I still am. Even though I spent four years at college, I never left my mother. During my first year, she stayed in a nearby apartment for five months to make sure I was okay. I think about it now, and I laugh."

In his parents' marriage, there was possibly some dissatisfaction with the marital relationship, leading John's mother to form a coalition with her son. The normal triad became a strong dyad. She found it easier to handle John, who gladly cooperated with her to receive her increasing attention. She adored John, the perfect son, and developed feelings similar to the ones she had for her husband when she was first married. Both mother and son fed into each other's fantasies. John, on one of his mother's birthdays, went as far as to shop at Victoria's Secret, where he bought her a sexy bikini and a bra.

It is interesting to note what happens to many married couples. Initially they have a good relationship and get along just fine—until the advent of a child. They handle their dyadic relationship as spouses with little or no difficulty. The climate changes with the introduction of a third member. In some families, the original spousal relationship is never regained.

The father steps back to allow more involvement between mother and child. The mother becomes preoccupied with the infant, and the father may compensate by becoming more involved in extra-familial matters. For example, he may work harder to become a better provider.

In a later session, John divulged that when his mother had an eye operation, he had to come home from college and stay with her for a couple of weeks. He said that his own sight was badly affected, which caused a setback in his studies— *obviously he identified with his mother's ailment.*

We become aware that John was paying the price for his dependency on his mother, which she encouraged; it was an emotional death within life. John, the afflicted participant, was prepared to throw away almost everything of value in order to maintain an imaginary state of *containment* and keep everybody happy. The unconscious motivation was evident. The belief that he was *cured,* deceived him. When he finally decided to continue with his therapy, he had the following dream:

> *I was visiting my mother and father, who were in different wards in a hospital. I said to them, "Why can't you be together?" I moved their beds until they were side by side.*

This dream marked the first mention of his father. Moreover, it revealed much concerning his vital childhood relationships. John's relationship with each of his parents and their relationship to each other were emotionally and physically sick. John had experienced them apart and took it upon himself in his dream to bring them closer together. This unconscious desire to reconcile his parents gave evidence of his attempt to reinstate his father as a potent figure of his inner life.

In subsequent sessions, John began to refer to his father in positive terms. With the unconscious aim of perpetuating the entwinement with his mother, he and his mother had had the need to see his father as useless and ineffectual. Together they conspired to denigrate and dismiss the parental marriage as an incompatible partnership; John could thereby compensate for his mother's lack of satisfaction with her husband. In John's eyes, her marriage had failed, and subconsciously he wanted to compensate by being devoted to his Mama.

I have witnessed unhappily married mothers who cling relentlessly to one or another of their children, projecting onto this unfortunate child unconscious fantasies, images of divinity or devilishness which smother the normal unfolding of the child's potential personality. These mothers are unable to define a relationship that simultaneously contains togetherness and separateness, and the ego development of the child becomes atrophied.

The emotionally unavailable father is often the common denominator in the personal history of people afflicted by psychological problems. It is the father who plays a specific and essential role as the mediator of the difficult transition from the womb to the world. Without the father's emotional support, it becomes almost insurmountably difficult for a child to be properly born and confirmed in his own identity and to negotiate the unavoidable separation from the mother, a prerequisite to a satisfactory adult heterosexual commitment.

The father-mother-child triangle influences and forms the patterns for all subsequent relationships. Triangles by their nature are unstable and tend to divide into coalitions of two members against the third. This tendency towards coalitions appears to exist in all cultures and societies. In spite of being the basic model for all triangular relationships, they are fraught with inherent problems and are extremely difficult for most people to handle.

While most humans prefer dyadic relationships, they necessarily find themselves caught up in triangles. Young children in particular seem to prefer the one-to-one dyadic relationship with their peers. They appear to have a difficult time dealing with more than one playmate at a time. They tend to pair and ostracize the third child. Triangles of children are more enduring when there is an organized game that adds structure and stability to the activity. Left to their own devices, however, three children playing together usually break down into two children intensely involved and the third child being pushed to the periphery.

Any parent will admit that, at times, it is easier to handle a child in the absence of the other parent. Briefly, we can reflect that when a child has to deal with only one parent, the child loses a leverage of manipulation and control over the other parent. When the other parent is added to form the triangle, the potential for manipulation increases immeasurably. Children are masters in pitting one parent against the other. *Divide and conquer* is one of the favorite games they play with parents. The child may make an alliance overture to one parent to gain favors and then use the same tactics with the other. It seems impossible for the primary triad to be stable and secure all the time for all the members concerned. One member of the triangle must always be in some state of *odd man (or woman) out*, unless the parents are united in their efforts to handle special situations.

If triangles form and shape many of our relationships and cannot be avoided, we can still maintain a healthy dyadic relationship without ignoring the potential of the triangle. In some situations I have witnessed, triangulations serve as survival techniques. The important issue is to maintain a reasonable harmony in the family; we need to be aware of the influence that each member exercises on one another.

Thoughts You May Consider

- Every son needs to realize that he is responsible for his own identity as a man. He is not chained to his parent's—or specifically, to his father's—attitudes and values. Every human being undergoes different physical and emotional changes. Like master sculptors, each one of us needs to chisel off parts of our character that could be harmful and give our personality desirable form, shape, and direction.
- Sometimes we set up a situation so that we may get a response resembling our experience with our father. If our father was a benevolent figure when we were growing up, then we seek benevolence in others. But if he was a hostile, emotionally detached man, we might seek that type of a person for a relationship. It is a familiar, if primarily unconscious, interaction. It serves

in part to recreate our past in order to correct it or cure our pain surrounding it.

- Before we pronounce any judgment against the emotionally absent father, we must carefully consider what has caused his lack of emotional availability. Under what conditions did he grow up? What kind of fatherhood did he experience in his early childhood? Was his father emotionally available to him? Was he affectionate to him? Did he play with him? Did he validate his presence in the family?

- When the one we label as absent father became a father, whose model of fathering did he have to follow? What if he had felt abandoned by his father? Now being married, did the mother of his child make an effort to involve him in parenting their newly-born child? Or did she focus her total attention on her child, oblivious to the needs of the father?

- After an inner personal inventory, the man—who is perceived as, or accused of being, the absent father— may realize that he has been emotionally unavailable to his child. And when he comes to his senses, he may seek reconciliation. That means consciously connecting with the supposed emotionally deprived child. The process of reconciliation takes effort and time, but gradually it brings great relief and harmony to the family.

4

When Mothers Are Absent

In our life we meet broken people, abandoned children, neglected parents, women left behind, and men despondent. In most cases these broken humans are asking, "Why do I feel like this?" If there was a way to put them face to face with themselves, they might discover new energy. The only way out of misery is found only in ourselves.

Do we ever separate emotionally from mother? Does mother ever separate emotionally from us? Physically we could live thousands of miles apart, yet emotionally we feel connected. Can a mother ever be absent from her child's life? Sometimes—but at any time of need, she is always present. If a mother dies when her child is still an infant, we wonder what emotional effect that has on the child. When a family loses the mother, the family feels unstable. However, when the father dies, the family unit is not threatened. If a family suffers the loss of a father, the mother takes over and the family manages to survive and cope with the sadness.

The Queen Mother will be remembered along with Churchill as the great leader in Britain's hour of need, comforting the nation during World War II in the face of Hitler's threat. And, of course, there was the Queen, providing stability throughout the dismantling of the British Empire. When Princess Diana died, Great Britain behaved with the hysteria of a motherless nation. If a family or an entire nation is affected by the loss of a mother figure, we can imagine the effect her absence would have on a person's emotional life.

✳ ✳ ✳

In her novel *The Secret Life of Bees,* Sue Monk Kidd tells the story of a little girl, Lily Owens, whose mother was killed when Lily was four years old. Lily shapes her entire life around that devastating, blurred memory—the afternoon her mother was killed. Since that time, her only real companion is the fierce-hearted black woman, Rosaleen, who acts as her "stand-in mother."

Overwhelmed with feelings of sadness, anger, and guilt, and realizing for the first time how little she really knows about her mother, Lily begins an obsessive search for answers—answers to the many questions she asks her only available support. Will the satisfaction of finally uncovering the *truth,* against all the odds, be worth the price she will have to pay mentally and emotionally?

In search of memories of her mother, Lily finds herself in the only direction open to her. She and Rosaleen take off for a town called Tiburon in South Carolina. She found the name on the back of a picture among the few possessions left by her mother. During the months of May, June, July, and August, an eccentric trio of black, beekeeping sisters takes them in. Lily enters their mesmerizing secret world of bees and honey. Maternal loss and betrayal, guilt and forgiveness lead Lily to the single thing her heart longs for most—finding the truth of how her mother died.

Holding Lily's hand, August says, "You have to find a mother inside you yourself. We all do. Even if we already have a mother, we still have to find this part of ourselves inside. She is the power inside you, you understand? Not only the power but the love." August offers words of a rare wisdom about life – about mothers and daughters and the women in our lives who become our true mothers. She speaks about the divine power of women and the transforming power of love.

❊ ❊ ❊

As we try to analyze the concept of Mother, it is like analyzing the existence of God. Both are mysteries. When we think of God, we Christians perceive Him as a caring Father, Creator of all visible things, Sustainer of the Universe. We may describe the attributes of God as loving, powerful, and compassionate—forces that keep the universe in motion and in harmony, making our hearts tick and keeping us alive.

As we think ideally of Mother, how do we perceive her? An instant response may be: *She is a source of love and care, compassion and patience. She is God's right hand. Without her presence, there would be no life on this planet. She is a co-creator and sustainer of a smaller universe, the family. "God could not be everywhere, and therefore He made mothers," claims a Jewish proverb.*

In his quest for the Oval Office, U.S. President Barack Obama became aware of his perspective on the world. After his mother's death, he saw the fallacy of focusing on the impact of his absent father, ignoring the greater impact of his ever-present mother, until her death made her absent as well. How sad that often we have such a tendency.

Most women are unaware of the importance of motherhood until after they become mothers. We take mother for granted, and sometimes we are oblivious to her contributions. When a woman becomes a mother, her power becomes invincible. There is a commitment to her destiny: *I am a mother. I know what my child needs.* She would sacrifice anything—even deprive herself of material luxuries or comforts—to raise healthy and happy children.

Visualize a mother holding a baby and entering a bus or a train filled to capacity with passengers. Simultaneously, all heads turn to look at mother and child. Why? My thoughts are that at the sight of mother, we instantly recollect those early stages of life, when mother held us affectionately in her arms and gave us that unconditional love. Without mother's loving care we could be dead, if not physically, then emotionally.

In view of the above description of mother, we are left with the psychological implication that we really never separate from mother. *There are circumstances in which a mother may be absent either emotionally or physically, but her child, regardless of age, never feels separated from her.* For conscious or unconscious reasons, there are times when a mother breaks away from her child. Such a break has a definite effect upon the child.

This was the case of **Philip**, an eight-year-old boy with swarthy complexion, curly hair, and big black eyes, who suffered the consequences of a divorce. His parents had divorced for two years when his mother left town to live with another man whom she planned to marry. In those two years, she had no contact with her son. She felt it was her son who kept her stuck with her husband in a bad marriage. "Phil can be raised by his father," she said. In her eyes, the child represented the father; he was a carbon copy of his father, and to the extent that she hated the father, she hated the child. The child's identity was denied because of her strong negative feelings toward his father.

As Philip entered his teen years, he learned to use defense mechanisms to protect himself and to conceal the fact that his mother had abandoned him. These mechanisms were psychological tricks he played upon himself to lessen the pain. It hurt to admit that his mother had abandoned him. One of these defense mechanisms was repression. He buried the feelings of abandonment deep in his heart, but lurking feelings of rejection continued to influence his behavior. He sought solitude, stayed in his room that he decorated with posters of heroes, and listened to brass music. In school he did poorly and wanted to drop out and join a musical band.

Nancy, a fourteen-year-old, good-looking blonde whose parents divorced, blamed her mother for not being able to maintain a relationship with her father. She moved into her father's apartment and played the surrogate wife, cooking and decorating, doing jobs her mother failed to do. Her mother, frustrated with Nancy's decision, began to recollect memories of Nancy's earlier life with her father. She, as a wife awaiting the return of her husband each evening, always found herself in second place because her four-year-old daughter ran around her and leaped into her daddy's arms. For a minute or two, her husband responded to his daughter with warmth and affection, and then he would turn to greet his wife. Her covert jealousy and resentment grew over the years to the point of rage.

When her father began to date and bring a girlfriend to his apartment, Nancy was caught on the horns of a dilemma. She felt replaced by daddy's girlfriend. Although she valued the freedom and independence she had enjoyed with her father, now she wanted to return to her mother's home. She yearned for love and acceptance and felt that her mother would be happy to have her back. Her mother, having recovered from the trauma of the divorce and being happily re-married, relinquished her negative feelings and welcomed her daughter. She put the welfare of her daughter above her personal interests. Her generosity to Nancy was above the call of duty, and she was able to dismiss her negative feelings. Now as two mature adults, the mother overcame her repressed rage, and the daughter let go of her feelings of abandonment. They reconciled in a spirit of mutual love and forgiveness.

A problem arises when an abandoned person who starves for love and acceptance enters married life. If both mates are abandoned persons, their expectations and demands of one another lead to frustration, anger, and disappointment. In married life, the abandoned person's need for attention, acceptance, and affection is constant. This puts a great burden on the other spouse. When the spouse is unable to respond at times with the same intensity of affection as the abandoned spouse expects, the spouse feels abandoned again. He or she may become depressed, angry, or hurt and make even more demands on the other mate for love and acceptance.

Abandonment or betrayal is the perception of a child who is orphaned at an early age. **Eric** had no memory of his parents. A grandmother raised him from the time he was three years old. Both of his parents were killed in a car accident, and his father's mother took care of him. In spite of his grandmother's loving care, Eric nurtured the feeling of abandonment.

Thirsting for love and validation, when he became twenty-six Eric married Jennie, whom he had dated for three years. His wife provided a good home and loved him dearly. In spite of her loving care and affections, however, Eric subconsciously questioned his wife's love. Even her slightest irritation or unavailability, unrelated to him, was interpreted as lack of love.

"I don't think you really care how I feel," he said. "I'm trying to please you, and you ignore my efforts. I don't think you love me."

"You can believe what you want to believe," Jennie replied, angered at his doubt. "Either you take my relationship with you at face value, or you don't. I don't know how else I can prove that I love you."

Although, Jennie's frustration was justified, the confrontation threw Eric back to the feeling of emotional abandonment, and he avoided any further dialogue with her. He could not appreciate his wife's love and devotion, aspects that could bridge the gap of his parental absence. The relationship suffered, and eventually he decided to divorce his wife in the hope that he could find another woman who could love him as he thought he deserved.

Eric still had to learn the origins of his feelings of abandonment that gradually surfaced in his marriage. He felt abandoned by his parents, and subconsciously he abandoned his wife and himself. As a result, they both felt abandoned.

※ ※ ※

Sarah, 32, a college graduate and a successful woman in the corporate world, was two years old when her mother died. Her father remarried, and Sarah was raised by a stepmother who was strict and punitive. In her early twenties, when she finally moved out and had her own apartment, she began to wrestle with feelings of abandonment. She had a very difficult time with people. She had dated several young men, but her relationships were superficial and short. A man she dated for three years and whom she was hoping to marry left her for another woman. Months later, she came to see me. With a grimace of discomfort, she informed me why she sought therapy.

"In the past six months, I've been dating Larry, and I have never been so much in love in my life. We both feel the same way about each other. We visualize having a home and children, and we talk about spending the rest of our lives together. But deep down I have a fear that Larry is going to leave me. I had the same fear before about another man who had promised to marry me, and he left me."

"Why would Larry leave you if you love each other, as you said?"

"I think I have one issue that's creating the problem. When our relationship became serious and intimate, I began to ask Larry if he would ever leave me, and he constantly reassured me of his love for me."

At length, Sarah spoke about her fears of abandonment. She had real fears that Larry's feelings for her might change. When she described her formative years with her stepmother, I began to think that her fears were based on the fact that her real mother had died. In essence, she felt abandoned by her mother. Her stepmother was verbally and physically abusive. Although Sarah had several potentially good relationships during her college years, all had ended for undefined reasons. She admitted that some of these relationships had ended because she felt the other person would stop loving her. This was her fear about Larry.

"If you are lovable and loving to Larry, why would he stop loving you?" I asked.

"I don't know. I'm reaching a point where I'm afraid to make plans even with my friends because I don't want my feelings to be hurt."

"I wish I could promise you that you'll go through life without ever being hurt or hurting someone," I said.

In my practice, I have counseled certain people who had felt abandoned by their mothers, either by death or by divorce, and who had chosen marriage partners who would likely abandon them. Subconsciously, they repeat what they experienced as children. They are familiar with the same kind of distance and mistreatment or emotional deprivation they experienced in childhood. They don't realize that they will never receive sufficient love and approval from someone who, by their own inadequacies and deficiencies, have little or nothing to give. It is like going to a dry fountain for water. People with abandonment issues question everyone's intentions, even those that are close to them.

Thoughts You May Consider

- Solutions for abandoned or rejected persons can be found for a spouse, sibling, relative, or friend. Solutions provide elementary support that gradually wears out but paves the way for healing. A therapist may offer significant help, but eventually, it is God who provides the ultimate comfort and peace.
- Some people prefer not to be in relationships and prefer to be lonely, though it hurts, because they are afraid of something that hurts even more—rejection. If we wish to be emotionally healthy and be at peace with our inner selves, fostering relationships can be the answer, as we learn to appreciate another person's strengths and weaknesses.
- Remembering that we are really in the sight of God can, in time, overshadow the negative memories from the past and fill the gap that parental absence left behind. There is tremendous relief in knowing that God's love for us is utterly unconditional.

- In spite of emotional deficiencies, we have a sense of security, as we believe that the Holy Spirit abides within us. *My children, I will not leave you orphans.... I will send you the Paraclete, the Comforter,* Jesus said to his disciples (John 15:12). The Holy Spirit, who abides within us, is our source of strength throughout our earthly life, helping us to face difficulties and fulfill our needs.

- If the fear of abandonment is lingering within you and is hindering your ability to achieve happiness in life, rest assured that it can be treated with therapy as long as you are willing to use a therapist or a spiritual counselor as a trusting mentor until you find peace in your life. Abandonment or rejection cannot be self-treated. As you connect with a loving person and develop a genuine relationship, healing is possible.

5

In Search of a Loving Father

Fathers play a crucial role in their children's perceptions. Whether we realize it or not, our fathers have made a lasting impression on us. Whether they were close or distant, present or absent, cold or warm, loving or abusive, our fathers have left a mark on our life and continue to influence our lives today—probably more than we are willing to admit.

Two reasons have motivated me to write this book: First, over the many years that I have practiced psychotherapy, I have seen countless clients whose unhappiness and lack of personal fulfillment lay in the memory of a bad relationship with their father. He was absent or emotionally unavailable or not interested in the growth of his child. Second, at the beginning of my practice I came across an old Chinese proverb that I have adopted as my personal credo:

> *If there is righteousness in the heart, there will be beauty in the character.*
> *If there is beauty in the character, there will be harmony at home.*
> *If there is harmony in the home, there will be order in the nation.*
> *When there is order in each nation, there will be peace in the world.*

Behind the idea of the personal father whom we know and to whom we relate lies an innate psychological image that influences the way we experience the father. This image functions as a blueprint or barometer of different aspects of our daily life. This image of the father leads us to experience events and people in a patterned way. When we relate to the father, we relate also to our expectations of him. He is strong or weak, stifling or facilitating, depending on how he does or does not fit in with our expectations.

At an early age, children are faced with a father image that is exaggerated and one-sided. *My father can do everything!* The father is idealized. As they grow and recognize the human elements in the father and gradually see the father as he really is, then begins their dissatisfaction with their relationship with him. At best they judge him critically, at worst they avoid contact with him. Under this avoidance lurks the thirst for a loving father.

The fact remains that growing up is costly, and the father's contribution is most valuable. If he is perceived as too strong of a father, he quells the child's independent spirit. If he is weak, he leaves his child unprotected and unmotivated. An all-facilitating father is not a good introduction to life. An all-harsh father, a critical and castrating man, wreaks havoc in the psychosocial development of his child.

In our times, although many fathers participate in the birthing of a child, the father's presence is sometimes initially viewed as an interruption of the mother-infant relationship. Mother is the immediate principle of bonding. If the infant is to develop into a whole person, the father must take part in the maternal oasis, the mother-child relationship. The father has to be active and insert himself between mother and baby as a reminder of the world outside their relationship.

One aspect that needs to be observed is the degree of rivalry that may surface during parenting. Sometimes the identity of a parent becomes tangled up with a worry that he or she may not be the *special* parent of the baby; a covert competition may begin between father and mother, both for loving the baby and for winning the baby's love. Parents experiencing the rivalry are expressing unmet needs to feel special, needs stemming from their own childhood. Fathers may have to accept that there are things they cannot do for their babies, and then they may feel less guilty about their contribution. A father-mother team can actually serve the best interests of the child. *While mother provides loving nurture, father provides challenge and support.* If motherly love is considered as unconditional love in its early stages, fatherly love is conditional. *I love you because you fulfill my expectations, because you look like me, or because I have plans for you when you grow up.*

One of the significant issues in human life is the separation the child experiences through the process of separating from the mother. Between the fifteenth and eighteenth month, the child seeks a sense of autonomy and responds to mother with a loud *No!* It is most important for the child to be allowed to say *no,* so that the baby may experience his or her individuality. Nature pushes the baby to be a separate person. A wonderful process to witness is a child's growth away from the symbiotic relationship with the mother.

As the child begins the process of separation, the father may play a significant part. In actuality, both parents can help the child gain self-reliance and autonomy. Parents need to allow the child to say *no,* gently direct its movements, and help establish boundaries. Fathering helps the child move on, explore new territories, and contact the world.

(The fathering principle here must be understood as psychological fathering, not biological. Conceivably, a woman can and in many situations does provide adequate fathering. Most psychotherapists are able to provide substantial evidence that our psychologically troubled world is in dire need of psychological fathering.)

Many books and articles, scholarly and secular, give ample evidence of the mothering principle—healthy and supportive mothering or unhealthy and destructive mothering. The attempt here is to explore and develop the fathering principle so that we understand its contribution to human development.

Fathering consists of certain healthy components that complement mothering and help the child grow into a complete person. These components, available also to the mother, are protecting, loving, caring, teaching, and introducing the world to the child. It involves bonding that pulls the child's world together and away from the mother. Balanced human growth implies that both mother and father are present in a child's life to model love, caring, and intimacy, and each one contributes a part to the child's completeness. For example, a boy learns what it takes to be a man from his father. He cannot learn this adequately from his mother. A girl needs a mother to model for her what it takes to be a woman. The girl also needs to experience a deep connection to her father, an experience that manifests erotic signs (in the psychological sense of the word). If this does not take place, then the father cannot initiate his daughter into the next stage of her development. Many fathers and daughters fail to achieve this link for fear of conveying the wrong message. A mother has experienced a closer and earlier physical bond with all her children and hence is less anxious about her own incestuous impulses. The father's failure to participate in a mutual attraction and mutual renunciation of (psychologically) erotic fulfillment with his daughter deprives her of psychological growth. Over-strictness or indifference can result in mockery of her sexuality. The father's contribution as a loving and caring male who respects his daughter's sexuality helps the daughter see herself as a sexually attractive adult. The restrictive and unemotional father causes his daughter to lose sight of her viability as a female. In the case of a son, he may develop an attitude that men have no emotions.

The decline of fatherhood is a major force behind many of the most disturbing problems that plague our society. The absence of a father or his lack of interest in his children is a contributing factor to the increasing criminal behavior of boys and the sexual activity and pregnancy of teenage girls.

✳ ✳ ✳

Cindy, a beautiful sixteen-year-old, became pregnant by a fifteen-year-old boy whom she used to help with homework. Her divorced mother encouraged abortion. The pain and guilt that followed the abortion caused Cindy to find refuge in her aunt's house in another state. Currently in her mid-thirties and having had a few unsuccessful relationships, Cindy is still searching for a mate with fatherly qualities.

Cindy's situation is not unique. Many teenage girls find themselves pregnant and compelled to have an abortion, causing incredible pain to themselves and to their families. Teen alcohol, truancy, and drug abuse continue to be epidemic. Had these children received healthy and loving fathering at home, chances are they would not have fallen from grace. Few people doubt the fundamental importance of mothers, but what of fathers and their role? If their contribution is minimal, it may be the result of an absent father who is either busy climbing the ladder of success, or a father considered a second adult in the home. Some assertive and capable wives take over major family responsibilities and indirectly train their husbands to be an *older son*. When fathers lose their importance as models of male behavior, their sons look for heroes to emulate, but heroes as portrayed in the movies may be so dauntingly powerful they overwhelm rather than inspire. Another reality of concern is that in recent years single parenting has become popular, is considered a form of heroism, and is often praised. Living in a fatherless household poses hazards for children.

Evelyn, a high-school dropout, felt abandoned by her father and angry with her mother, who could not hold on to her husband. Evelyn left her home on her eighteenth birthday without leaving a note for her divorced mother. She was the only daughter, and from the time of her parent's divorce when she was thirteen years old, she was troubled. At that time, she came to my office for counseling, but after three visits she did not return. She resisted any positive directives. Ten years later, she made an appointment to see me again. She said she remembered me, but when I saw her I did not recognize her at all. Her face was a mass of wrinkles, and streaks of gray hair made her look old. She held a restless toddler in her arms, trying to keep him quiet as she related her story of a second pregnancy with a man she had planned to marry. He disappeared without a trace. She admitted that she was in treatment for drug addiction.

The files of psychotherapists and marriage and family therapists are filled with stories similar to those of Evelyn and Cindy. A significant issue in each life is painfully failed relationships with men or difficulty connecting with the right mate. Both are in search of a loving father to take care of them and protect them from the perils of life. The issue underlying their problems is a deep need, a cry for a father's love. Psychotherapists tell us that many dramas could be avoided if good and responsible fathers were present.

Timothy was eight years old when his father died. He keenly felt the loss of his father, and every Saturday he became depressed as he saw other boys going to a ball game with their fathers. His mother never remarried, but she found comfort in being the caretaker of her young son. Tim, as she called him, grew up among women: his mother's sister and his grandmother. During his growing years, he learned and internalized different female characteristics. Being much loved and protected by women, he learned to be always polite to them so he could benefit by their graces. Sports and male games were of no interest to him. He loved to play the violin to entertain his mother's girlfriends, and he took pride in doing house chores to please his mother. Through his college years and adult life he lived at home and was protective of his mother. She, in turn, enjoyed having him as the man of the house. She claimed that she wanted him to get married *to a nice girl*. Timothy rarely dated, and the girls he brought home, according to his mother, were not the right ones for him. Mother and son enjoyed each other's company, visiting friends, having dinners together, and traveling together. This type of loving mother-son relationship may be admired by some, but its normality is questionable. His mother died five years ago, and he, now in his mid-forties, lives alone. He claims that he wants to get married but that he seems unable to find the right mate. *Mama is no longer around to offer approval.* Many men who grow up without a father's presence or a caring male figure sacrifice their fulfillment and happiness. Usually, they take care of mother; on their part, some mothers thrive on having their sons at home.

There is no doubt that many women get along very well and raise their children without men in their lives. However, a marriage with two responsible spouses who love each other stands a better chance of providing a healthy environment for their children's upbringing. When a caring and compassionate atmosphere is absent from the home and children are neglected, it is easy to recognize the emotionally damaging effects. When father and mother are constantly quarreling angrily with each other, the children absorb and develop negative tendencies. Emotionally abandoned, they feel helpless and insecure, and their minds are often agitated. When parents disagree on certain issues in a civil way, although children may initially find this objectionable, eventually they come to understand it as normal. This learning can gradually be taken out of the home and into the world. As children receive frequent affection and protection, they tend to be happier, healthier, and more confident in their abilities.

Love between mother and father can be the basic dynamic that nurtures a child's healthy growth. Children are uncanny judges of their parents' relationship with each other. Because of this intuitive ability, a crucial realization in the life of a child is the understanding of whether or not the mother and father have affection for each other. Children who know that their parents enjoy each other's company have a sense of security that can be attained from no other source. Some human behavior may appear to children as absurd or cruel, but as long as they see that the two most important adults in their life love and care for each other, they are satisfied. With the strength of that understanding, they are less vulnerable to being wounded by the inevitable blows of childhood and adolescence. If love between the parents is not present, however, then nothing can replace it in children's minds. They are threatened by the ultimate absurdity: the two people that they most naturally love are unwilling to love each other.

Reversing the Tide

If fathers are to be reinstated in the lives of their children, the cultural shift of the last few decades towards radical individualism must be re-examined and corrected. Marriage must be re-established as a strong institution. Practical steps must be seriously considered. For example, companies and employers could provide generous parental leave and experiment with flexible work hours for parents. Religious leaders could reclaim moral ground from the culture of easy divorce and non-marriage. The temptation to equate committed relationships with official marriage should be discouraged. Marriage and family therapists could begin their sessions with a bias in favor of marriage, stressing the needs of the family at least as much as the needs of the client.

Divorce laws and judges could consider two realities: marriages without minor children could be relatively easy to dissolve, but marriages with children should be subject to stricter guidelines. Longer waiting periods for divorcing couples with children might be necessary, combined with mandatory marriage and family therapy. Divorce may end a marriage, but it does not end a relationship. Its impact continues to live on and haunt the survivors, especially the children. In my practice, I have yet to see children who were comfortable with their parents' divorce. Their endless *Whys* remain with only few reasonable answers. I have seen a large number of marriages of young people whose parents had divorced; these young people are quick to jump into divorce themselves, oblivious of the consequences. *My parents went through a divorce and survived and so can I. If my marriage doesn't work, I know what to do.*

If we are to progress toward a more just and humane society, we must reverse the tide that is pulling fathers from their families. Nothing is more important for our children or for our future as a nation than cohesive family units. A mother's part in promoting and supporting the importance of the father to his children is important. Understandably, mother loves the newborn infant because it is her child; it came totally out of her; she gave it flesh, bones, and life. Although the father's part may be different, this is the time that the father should not be ignored. The mother must invite the father to be an intimate part of this blessed event and rejoice in the birth of their infant.

All this amounts to a reality that bringing up children is demanding, stressful, and exhausting, and requires responsibility. Children from single-parent families are twice as likely to drop out of school as those from healthy two-parent homes. Two mature adults can support each other. They can offset each other's deficiencies and build each other's strengths.

Fathers bring an array of unique qualities to a home. Some are familiar; fathers protect and role model. It is through solid fathering that men become truly men, able to give something back to others, rather than focusing their life on material success, seduction of women, and control tactics that make them feel manly. Fathering children of their own gives their lives meaning and purpose. Many a man finds it comfortable raising a son, involving him in his work and sports, and praising his ability. Teenage boys without fathers are notoriously prone to trouble. The pathway to adulthood for daughters is somewhat easier, but they must also learn from their fathers how to relate to men in ways they cannot learn from their mothers. They learn from their fathers about heterosexual trust and intimacy. They learn to appreciate their own femininity from the one male who is most special in their lives. Most important, through loving and being loved by their fathers, they learn that they are love-worthy. A father who wants his daughter to be strong, mentally healthy, and secure must like and respect his wife. His daughter's self-esteem depends on his attitude. If the father believes women are limited in what they can do in life, that women are weak and need to be protected by men, then his daughter is likely to grow up limited and weak. To a large degree, her successes in life and in love are in his hands. The image of their father that girls gradually internalize influences their choice of a mate.

In some situations the father's involvement seems to be linked to improved verbal and problem-solving skills and higher academic achievement. The presence of the father who is nurturing the growth of his children is one of the determinants of the proficiency of boys and girls in mathematics, verbal ability, and intelligence. The benefits of active fatherhood encourage boys to develop characteristics, including prudence, cooperativeness, honesty, trust, and self-sacrifice—qualities that can lead to achievement as an economic provider. Having children typically impresses upon men the importance of setting a good example. Even some of the mischievous and rebellious characters who lived an irresponsible life as bachelors go through a radical transformation when they marry and have children. They sober up and become exemplary fathers.

Thoughts You May Consider

- Ideally a loving father is physically, emotionally, and intellectually available. He possesses a series of qualities and capacities that provide the child with experiences over a period of time until the child becomes an adult.
- Growing children are not aware of the demands they make on the father. What they are aware of is the feeling of frustration or annoyance they experience when the father does not meet their demands. It is questionable at what point of their lives children accept their fathers for who they are—humans with strengths and weaknesses.
- When children become adults, and maturity sets in, they may be able to accept, be more compassionate, and forgive their fathers. If fathers are perceived as having done nothing for their children, the fact remains that at least they caused their birth.
- Those who have only painful memories of their fathers can turn to another secure source of unconditional love, to God the Heavenly Father. Through faith and prayer they may gain a better understanding of who their fathers really were and what contribution the father made to them.
- Through his prophet Jeremiah, God speaks to all those who are in search of a loving father: *I have loved you, my people, with an everlasting love. With unfailing love I have drawn you to myself* (Jer 31:3). Our Heavenly Father never gives up on us. Regardless of our state of mind, He never stops loving us.

6

"Is There Someone
Who Can Love Me?"

*Love is the reality of our total self which we can repress or express. Unless we realize this truth, we may go on indulging in the romantic myth that someday love will happen to me. Love has never just happened to anyone. People spend years of trying to find love. But love is not to be **found**. It consists not in finding the right person who can love you, but in becoming the right person who could be loved.*

In reading the previous chapters, you have probably identified with aspects of life that are familiar to you. Questions may surface in your mind, and you may wonder: *Can there be any peace in my life? I have had my share of trouble. Can I find a little comfort somewhere? Can somebody love me?* Yes. If you want to find comfort and peace, you may have to accept this world as it is and do all you can to cultivate harmony within yourself and in your immediate environment. The key to gaining the balance between the world we live in and our personal convictions is to appreciate what is good and of benefit to our life today. If we attach ourselves to our ambitions or possessions, our image or status, we will experience increasing anxiety but no peace.

Is there a human being who can love me? you may ask. *Is there someone I could love?* Yes is the answer, provided that you are emotionally and physically available. Love is the simplest yet most important need for all humans. It is our basic longing to be the love object and to be able to give love back. We need love as we need air to breathe, water and food, and sun and rain. Without these we would perish. No other need is quite so significant to our nature.

These and other questions that the previous chapters have raised are good and normal for people in their quest for happiness. If we were to encapsulate all these questions into one word, that word would be *Love*. Most of our efforts in life reveal that the deep yearning of the human heart is to be loved, to love, and to heal.

Historian Arnold Toynbee said, *I think that love is the only spiritual power that can overcome the self-centeredness that is inherent in being alive. Love is the thing that makes life possible or, indeed, tolerable.* For many, life is intolerable because they do not believe anyone really loves them. Yet God proclaims His unconditional love for every one of us. God wants us to understand that He loves us and He wants us to receive His love. Our part is to share His love with others. Hear His words as recorded in St. John's Gospel, chapter 13:34–35.

> *A new command I give you. Love one another. As I have loved you, so you must love one another. By this, all humanity will know that you are my disciples, if you love one another.*

When our self-image is tarnished and we feel abandoned, alone, lonely, or rejected, we fear that we will never be accepted or loved. *Nobody cares for us.* Yet we survive with the hope that there is at least one person in the world who will accept us and love us anyway. This comforting fantasy, that someone out there will love us unconditionally all the time, can sustain us for a long time. *And when we find that person and feel loved, we will be happy.* I have seen several people who continue to seek someone special who will sweep them off their feet and save them from the chaos that is within them. Basically, they feel inadequate and unworthy of love, and yet they hope against hope that there is that person who truly is capable of loving them and making them worthy. It is a romantic notion to believe that such a person exists, or that out there somewhere there is unconditional love. That type of love, only God can provide. Seriously, *is there such a person whose love is unconditional?* That is only an attribute of God. *He sends rain on the just and the unjust equally.*

Lucky is the person who experiences love in the presence of a friend or a spouse or a sibling. That love is conditional, and it needs to be reciprocal. When it is nurtured it paves the way to a more meaningful and better relationship. It is then that we realize the presence of God in our midst. God has loved us first and endowed each one of us with this type of love to enable us to reconnect in a godly manner with other people and significant others in our life. A whole city can be in total darkness if its electric system is not connected to the main generator, the source that produces electricity. God's gift of love cannot be appropriated unless we are connected to Him who is the source of love. His love is unconditional, non-possessive, and non-demanding. It requires obedience to love Him and to love one another. He wants to see us happy with each other by loving.

Granted that it is difficult and unrealistic to love everybody or to be loved by everyone. That is why we have difficulty in giving an adequate definition of love. There is no word in our language that is used with more meanings than the word *love*. Most meanings are incomplete in that they hide the true underlying motives and feelings. The brutal frankness of Charlie Brown's friend Linus is hilarious because it is so true to life: *I love mankind—it's **people** I can't stand.* You and I can redefine the practice of love by being loving. In respecting and loving ourselves properly we learn to respect and love others. We can always keep in mind that love is not finding the right person to love or to be loved by. It is *being* the right person to love. Like the sun behind the clouds, there is always love behind our present condition—if we are to turn it on by being loving.

Dostoevsky in his description of *The Brothers Karamazov*, writes:

> *Love all of God's creation, the whole and every grain of sand in it. Love every leaf, every ray of God's light. Love the animals, love the plants, love everything. If you love everything, you will perceive the divine mystery of things. Once you perceive it, you will begin to comprehend it better every day. You will come at last to love the whole world with an all-embracing love.*

Then, with Linus, you will declare, *I love all humankind.* But unlike him, you will add, *And I love all people as I love myself. I love others, even if they treat me unfairly. I love them, not because they deserve love, but because I do—for life is for loving.*

This powerful force we call love already exists within us. Perhaps you have not experienced love, either because in your early years you did not feel sufficiently loved, or because you were ignored, rejected, or abandoned in the hands of a stranger. Yet the seed of love was already in your heart. It is still there within you. Think about it. Although untapped, dormant, or repressed, it can perform miracles if it is activated. We are born to be loving people. You and I want to be loving, but each person needs to learn to love by practice. The experience of love is a choice we make, a mental decision to see love as the only real purpose and value in life. Love in your mind produces love in your life. Love implies action. If we do not know how to drive a car or how to swim, reading books or watching TV shows about driving or swimming can be of no benefit.

Love is a spiritual experience. It is God's special gift to every human being. God wants us to be in fellowship with Him. That was the reason for His incarnation. He became human, in no way different from other human beings, and went through every stage of human development to break through the walls of power in total weakness. That is the story of Jesus. He was born in a stable—not in the modern Christmas stable we see in full color and lights, displayed in department stores, but in a reeking, dark, four-walled home for animals. His first cradle was the manger where the animals chewed their cud. It was not by chance that Christ was born in a stable. The powerlessness of the manger climaxed on the cross as he subjected himself to humility and ridicule. He did not try to prove the power of his divinity. Instead, he demonstrated the reality of human powerlessness. People who had witnessed his miracles, his loving and compassionate life, shouted sarcastically: *He saved others; He cannot save Himself. He is the King of Israel; let him come down from the cross now, and we will believe in Him* (Matt 27:42).

Abused by his enemies, rejected by his friends, and tortured by anguish, his spirit was shrouded in the darkness of abandonment. In his human nature, he felt abandoned, but his abandonment served a purpose. It was a comprehensive definition of life. Pain and suffering are inevitable parts of it. As we grow into childhood or adolescence, it is almost inevitable that we will be wounded in some way. An unscarred childhood is possible but rare. Life is difficult even when it appears wonderful. For many people, it is only difficult, not wonderful. At one time or another chances are that you were wounded. Perhaps one of your parents wounded you; if you were not wounded by your parents, you may have been wounded by the death or illness of a parent or sibling, a bitter marriage or divorce, the death of a friend or relative, an accident, or the failure of your first love—past issues may still linger unresolved. This does not mean that you are abnormal. You are only human, and psychotherapy can be of significant help. If physical wounds necessitate medical care, spiritual and psychological help can be of benefit to emotional wounds. But for a large number of people psychotherapy *alone* cannot solve all their problems. It paves the way to healing. The ultimate cure comes from God, the Healer of all afflictions and ills. He provides the ultimate cure.

Christ's cross offers strong evidence of comfort when we go through painful times. He transformed the meaning of suffering and made it part of His work of salvation. His death paid for our sins, but his resurrection reopened the gates of heaven. Death has no more dominion over our life.

When we face adversities and things do not go as we expected, we get angry. We look for someone to blame, we wonder how we got into difficult situations, and we question God's existence. We feel devastated, disturbed, abandoned. It seems that we are going through our own Good Friday, our *crucifixion*. So it seems. But what if we were to think for a moment of our Lord's death? What was the cry while on the cross? *My God, my God, why have you forsaken me?* His own disciples who had followed him for three years, who had witnessed his miracles and felt his love, abandoned him throughout his trial and death. Although he felt abandoned, he left with us a reality about life. There is cruelty, injustice, lack of love and forgiveness, pride, greed, gossip, addictions, and hypocrisy. We have to accept the possibility of these, simply because they are true, and we need to know the truth, learning to combat and overcome it by doing good and having honest intentions. Truth and love are God's attributes which He wants us to have in our life that we may face reality.

As we get deeper into ourselves, we become aware of the difference that God makes in our life, and how He makes his presence known to us with each breath we take. St. Paul told the sophisticated Athenians, *In him we live and move and have our being.* As we believe in God's presence in our life, we walk in a spirit of humility but with faith, confidence, and courage because we live under His grace. I often wish I had lived at that time and associated with those friendly folks who followed Him from place to place, eager to be in His presence and hear His voice.

It so happened that before I started writing this chapter, my wife Pat and I had the opportunity to go to Israel. What we saw and experienced in the old city of Jerusalem, where Christ's life and ministry began, was a most inspiring journey.

Do you want to be profoundly aware of Christ's presence, in touch with him at the deepest possible level, gleaning from his teachings and wisdom, and living as close to him as is humanly possible? Then, in the next few minutes, join me now that Jerusalem is fresh in my mind.

A Trip to Jerusalem

Mentally, follow me. Together let's walk uphill along the winding, narrow paths of the Holy Land; visualize Christ, listen to His voice, witness His caring and healing ministry, and sense His divinity through the countless miracles He performed.

Initially, we meet Jesus as a twelve-year-old speaking in the temple in Jerusalem. Curious and strange faces surround Him in wonder: Elders, high priests, and teachers of the law are amazed at his wisdom. They ask serious questions, and he answers with confidence and wisdom.

On another occasion, after a long hidden life in Nazareth, we meet Jesus again as he is about to begin his ministry. He starts with a self-portrait telling where He comes from and laying the foundation of His plan. The fifth chapter of Matthew's Gospel tells us what we can visualize:

When Jesus saw the crowds, He went up the mountain,
and after He sat down, His disciples came to him. Then
He began to speak, saying:

Blessed are the poor—Jesus identified Himself with those who are not in control, who are marginal in society, and whose pride is poor. The origins of His human nature are humble, and He comes into the world for them. The elite of His time question His motives. What knowledge could a person from Nazareth have?

Blessed are the gentle—Jesus does not break the bruised reed. He always shows compassion and cares for a little one whose heart is receptive like a little child. *You cannot enter the Kingdom of Heaven unless you have the heart of innocent children.*

Blessed are those who mourn—Jesus indicates that He does not hide His grief for the afflicted, the grieving, and suffering. He lets His tears flow when His friend Lazarus dies and when He foresees the destruction of His beloved Jerusalem.

Blessed are those who hunger and thirst for justice—Jesus does not hesitate to criticize injustice, hypocrisy, and greed, and He defends the hungry, the dying, and the lepers.

Blessed are the merciful—Jesus does not call for revenge or punishment but forgives the wrongdoer and heals those in pain and suffering.

Blessed are the pure in heart—Jesus remains focused only on what is necessary and does not allow His attention to be divided by distractions. One has to be pure in heart to experience God's love.

Blessed are the peace makers—Jesus does not stress differences nor does He discriminate; He reconciles people as brothers and sisters in one family.

Blessed are those who are persecuted—Jesus does not expect success and popularity, but He realizes that rejections and abandonment cause suffering—which will make Him suffer.

The Beatitudes, or How to Be-Attitudes, summarize a reality of human life, a glimpse of what Jesus had to go through during His earthly life. In essence, He wants us to know what to expect when we visit the sick, the wronged, prisoners, refugees, the hungry, the lonely, victims of emotional or sexual abuse, the dying—a common lot for all humans. But He is ever-present in everyone's life. It is His presence that gives purpose and meaning to those who suffer; and to the dead He grants life. As we walk with Him we hear amazing stories and messages coming out of His mouth. We witness miracles He performs to reveal God's power and to bring healing and joy to people's life.

We can continue our mental journey in the Holy Land and find the sights where Jesus, Son of God, revealed Himself in human flesh, taught lifetime lessons, healed the sick, and performed miracles. Finally we see Him on His way to Jerusalem, knowing that He will be betrayed, judged, mocked, tortured, and eventually crucified on the hill of Golgotha.

Walking through *Via Dolorosa,* the road along which Christ carried His cross, we see a dungeon carved out of stone; it is the prison where Jesus was kept before the crucifixion. Then we see Golgotha and the tomb. It is hard to describe all the steps of Jesus. They are preserved as holy shrines which thousands of people from around the world visit to confirm and revitalize their faith in Jesus Christ.

This imaginary visit to the Holy Land suffices to serve as a warm invitation to pick up your Bible, specifically the books of the New Testament where our Lord's life is recorded. It is a treasure of inspiration in our times when messages of annihilation constantly haunt our ears. Christ is our true companion, our guide and our God. He enriches our daily life with courage, compassion, and unconditional love.

Thoughts You May Consider

- Believing in God, Creator of the Universe, and Giver of Life is most empowering. We can see and admire God's creation and the order of the universe. We can be aware of our thoughts about human life from birth to death, our development, and our potential. Then we can ask: *What is this creative power and where does it come from, making our life a reality?*
- Being aware of how to interact with other people is important. Do we try to impress them? Do we need their attention? Do we judge them by appearance, or do we try to perceive what is behind their physical self—a human being created after the image and likeness of God? In a genuine relationship, there is an outward flow of open, alert attention toward the other person. We can learn to accept and love the other, as God accepts and love us.

- Defining ourselves by copying others or by opinions others may have about us can stifle our growth and maturity. If others insist upon defining who you are, they may be projecting how they feel about themselves. It is important to know how we feel about ourselves. Negative thinking or habits that we have can be chiseled off. We can develop positive aspects of our personality if want to regain peace of mind and inner contentment.

- Most people seek to be happy and make happiness their lifetime goal. How we attain a state of happiness is a serious issue. Accumulation of wealth and material possessions can make us happy for a while, but gradually the feeling of happiness fades. External things do not guarantee happiness. We need to be content with what we have each day and be free from unhappiness in order to experience well-being and inner peace, the source of true happiness.

- Jesus begins each of the Beatitudes with the word *Blessed*. The original word in Greek is *Makarioi,* the plural form of *Makarios*, which means *happy*. Jesus confirms God's wish that we should be happy. He placed Adam and Eve in Paradise, a place of ultimate bliss. But in disobeying God, they lost the potential of lasting happiness. God put us on this planet in a world of abundance to enjoy and be happy. Sometimes behaving with an angry or arrogant attitude, we disconnect ourselves from God. Once we make a turn and seek God's presence in our life and accept his forgiveness, we feel the profound joy of reconciliation, inner joy, peace, and connectedness with God.

7

Loneliness

There is no easy way leading us out of loneliness or delivering us with a little effort to a desired place. Although there will be companions along the route, the journey is one each of us must take ourselves. The journey itself and the companions we choose, the sharing of struggles and pain along the way, are the first steps out of loneliness.

Abandonment results in feelings of loneliness. *What is loneliness?* Is it a feeling? Is it a state of mind? Is it an attitude? Or is it a normal part of the human condition? For different people, loneliness has different meanings. It is hard to describe exactly what it is, or how we come to feel this way. Perhaps we can ask a more specific question—*What is loneliness for you?*

Loneliness is an emotional state in which a person experiences a powerful feeling of emptiness and isolation. It is a feeling of being cut off from other people. It is, specifically, the inability or unwillingness to live with others. Lonely people often do not think much of themselves and experience a feeling of unworthiness. They presume that nobody would like to be with them. The slightest smile from someone seems a turn-on, however, and for a while they fantasize that this person could be a good friend.

Have you ever felt disconnected from a significant person in your life? Did you ever need to share a happy or sad event with a trusting person who would listen to you and understand you? Did you ever feel that you wanted to love or be loved by someone? Do you have a feeling that nobody really loves you or cares about you or that you have no real feelings for anybody? If your answer is *Yes* to any one of these questions, then you probably feel lonely. There is nothing wrong with feeling lonely; most of us periodically do.

Loneliness is neither a permanent state nor a bad emotion in itself. It can be viewed more accurately as a signal or indicator of important needs that are going unmet. Are you looking for someone or something to make yourself feel more complete? Do you sense emptiness within that needs to be filled? There are married individuals who feel lonely in their marriage. If marriage is the answer to loneliness, how do we account for so many divorces? Is being single and *free* an answer to loneliness? If so, why do so many single people want to be married?

In searching for the ideal mate, most singles feel that out there awaits their soul mate who will provide love, security, excitement, and inspiration: that someone could be supportive physically, emotionally, and even financially, to allow them to maximize their own life's potential. Is there such a human being in this world, an *ideal mate,* who could fulfill all of someone else's needs? No one in the world can do that! Single people, of course, aren't the only ones who believe there is someone out there capable of satisfying their every need. Married people who have been disappointed with their marriage indulge in fantasies; perhaps, they imagine, had they married someone else or changed their partner, they would have found the satisfaction they seek—as if the next mate would miraculously meet all their needs.

✳ ✳ ✳

Bernie wavered between his unfulfilling relationship with his wife of twenty-four years and the infatuation and newness of life he had been experiencing during the last six months with a younger woman, Cheryl. With a married daughter and a son in college, Bernie was consumed with thoughts of how to tell his children that he planned to leave their mother and start a new life. He told his wife that he no longer had loving feelings for her and he wanted out. When he broke the news to his daughter, hoping that she would understand, she responded in tears. *How could you think of such a thing? All my life I thought that you and mom had such a good relationship. She adores you. You're going to break her heart.*

In therapy he admitted that he had no desire to be married to his wife any longer. "She's a good woman and a good mother," he said. "I still love her, but I don't want to live with her."

"Why?" I asked, knowing that Bernie had feelings for another woman.

"Something is missing in our relationship," he said.

"Do you feel deprived because your wife cannot give you that something?"

"I think there is something more out there, and now that I'm approaching fifty I need to find it. I deserve better," he replied emphatically.

In later sessions it was evident that Bernie had been feeling lonely for a long time. When the children were still living at home, the conversations were about the children. Once the children became emancipated, the parents didn't find much to talk about. This is a familiar pattern with many couples facing the empty nest syndrome. Bernie slowly drifted apart from his wife and sought greener pastures. Little did he know that changing partners does not necessarily bring the satisfaction one seeks. It could, however, delay the awareness of a real solution. Emotionally, he had disconnected from his wife and his children. As the president of a company, he worked primarily alone and experienced a unique kind of loneliness as the head of the company. During the day Cheryl, his secretary, was at his side. Besides being most efficient with office work, she graciously made coffee for him or shared lunch and pleasant conversation with him on occasions. This diffused Bernie's loneliness, but only for a while. Once he returned home, his loneliness returned. He found reasons to go into his home office and check his e-mail or send a little romantic message to his Cheryl. Meanwhile, his wife occupied herself with housework or watched TV. Sensing Bernie's lack of interest, she asked him if there was a problem. His answer was brief. "I'm unhappy."

Of course, he did not tell his wife that in the last three months he'd been having an affair with Cheryl. Unable to avoid the temptation, Bernie found himself entrapped in a passionate affair and could not let it go. He had not expected it to go that far. "I can handle it," he thought, "and can still be married." But his secretary, in her late twenties, had her own thoughts. Her father was hostile, rejecting, and lacking affection, something she missed in teenage years. She remained with her mother, feeling abandoned and uncared-for by her father. In pleasing Bernie, her keen yearning for affection for an older, married man became manifest. Subconsciously, she was probably looking for a father.

Some affairs result in divorce, as Bernie's did. Did the affair cure his loneliness? Reader, don't you already know the answer to this question?

＊ ＊ ＊

You have heard about similar situations—they are common enough. They follow the usual pattern. You could fill in the rest of the story yourself, and you'd be close to what actually happened to the characters.

You may have been alone many times, but have you ever felt *lonely*? Lonely people feel as if they are in their own prison. They may be with other people, but they still feel alone. Deliberately, they cut themselves off from others, leaving themselves emotionally isolated. They have a hard time connecting with people, even with those who could be good friends. They are wary when someone tries to become closer, perhaps to pursue a friendship. Closeness and intimacy are threatening, so lonely persons build fences around themselves. They choose isolation.

Ironically, loneliness frequently occurs in heavily populated communities. There are inhabitants in big cities who feel utterly alone and cut off, even when surrounded by throngs of other people. Someone may come into daily contact with many individuals and routinely interact with them, yet she still feels cut off and alone. Quantity of contact does not translate into quality of contact.

✳ ✳ ✳

Jonathan was a university professor teaching mass media and communication skills in a graduate department. He and I had known each other for more than twenty years, and our families had socialized during major holidays. So he surprised me one day when in a man-to-man conversation he admitted that he was a lonely person, unable to have meaningful human contact. Although he was in frequent social and business situations with his associates, he acknowledged that often he experienced a subjective sense of inner emptiness and deep feelings of isolation. His single confidant was his wife. "I hold back personal thoughts and fantasies, for I'm afraid I might risk losing my wife's respect. I don't want to feel vulnerable."

As Jonathan confided more of his innermost feelings, he made me wonder how he could interact daily with colleagues and graduate students and still feel lonely. He had experienced no loss of any kind. He was highly respected in his field, and within his family he felt appreciated. It was unclear to me what the real source of his loneliness was. Did it stem from unrealized ambition at work or unrecognized appreciation at home?

In dealing with Jonathan's state of mind, the real issue of his loneliness became evident. When he was a child, he had had caretakers who had not been loving people. Most of the time they were inconsistent in their care of him, and as a result he became insecure with them; eventually he saw them as people not to be trusted. His emotions remained undeveloped because he did not receive proper emotional nourishment as a child. The lack of affirmation from significant others in his early life prevented him from developing a sense of his own worth, value, or goodness. Although a respected professor in his field, he had trouble opening up to the world around him.

Loneliness appears to have become an epidemic in modern times. There was a time when families were larger and more stable, divorce was less prevalent, and few people lived alone. Today, the trend is reversed. In our affluent society thousands of people seem to value a lifestyle of assumed independence and self-reliance. Young people, once they are financially stable, move out of their parents' home to live alone or with a roommate. Physical separation often weakens familial bonds, and nowadays, it is not at all unusual for a son or daughter to move to another part of the country or even the world, and be separated by hundreds or thousands of miles from their original homes.

Many of us suffer loneliness manifested in a number of ways. Loneliness can be seen in the need for conversation— even idle or silly—caused by the inability to connect with a caring friend. It can be seen in a need for constant entertainment: radio and TV sets are turned on for most of the day. iPods are often seen attached to our ears. Daily, hundreds of e-mails are exchanged among friends and acquaintances. Too much activity and surface talk, social events, and parties are used to fill up empty spaces: *Let's get together and do something or go somewhere and have fun so we won't be lonely.* Loneliness can play a part in alcoholism, sexual escapades, drug use, and antisocial or self-destructive behavior. These all have an effect on our ability to function in everyday life, to interact with other people honestly, to enjoy peace in our life, and even to enjoy a decent night's sleep.

There is nothing wrong with wanting to have fun, enjoying good company, or seeking entertainment, as long as we maintain a sense of responsibility, balance, and respect toward life. When we do not assess our own reality, we inevitably become alone. If we expect anyone else to take away our loneliness, we feel even lonelier.

It is important not to see loneliness as a sign of weakness or immaturity. There's nothing wrong with us if we experience periodic loneliness. It is a normal feeling precipitated by what we are thinking at a particular time. For example, at the end of the day, we are each alone. Can anyone ever truly understand what it is to be you, to experience all the things you have experienced, to understand your joys and happiness, your pains and sorrows? Surely we can talk to other people about how we feel; we can draw pictures, we can play music; but such attempts to communicate ultimately leave something out. We cannot always get our feelings, ideas, or experiences across exactly. Most of the time we censor them lest we be misunderstood. It is a painful reality that ultimately we are alone and often lonely. To feel lonely is to join the rest of humanity in acknowledging that we are somehow fundamentally separated from each other, with a choice to speak and yet never be fully understood. Loneliness can be made more intense by the way in which you define it. Avoid the misconception that loneliness results from a defect in your personality. If you tend to feel lonely frequently, examine your thoughts. What others think of you is not as important as what you think of yourself. Do not let negative thoughts alienate you from your own true self.

Living a life of uncertainty can cause loneliness. It is healthy to view loneliness as part of the essence of being human. Each human being comes into the world alone, travels through life as an individual, and ultimately dies alone. Coping with this, accepting it, and learning how to direct our own lives with some degree of grace and satisfaction are sound choices for each of us to make.

Thoughts You May Consider

- No matter how bad you feel, loneliness will diminish or even disappear when you focus your attention and energy on needs you can meet. Remember that loneliness is something that can be changed. Try not to view loneliness as a defect in personality or as an unalterable state of being.

- Loneliness is a common experience that can be changed the moment you begin to identify which of your needs are not being met. A good start can be to develop a circle of friends or one special friend with whom you can share personal interests.

- Intimate friendships usually develop gradually as people learn to share their inner feelings. Avoid rushing into intimate friendships by sharing personal issues too quickly or expecting that others will understand you completely in a short time. Let the process of friendship develop naturally. Value all of your friends and their unique characteristics rather than believing that only a romantic relationship could relieve your loneliness.

- Those who hide their loneliness from the outside world tend to become depressed. Remind yourself that your loneliness will not last forever. Put yourself in new situations where you will meet people. Engage in activities in which you have a genuine interest. In so doing, you will be more likely to meet the kind of people you are interested in meeting—people with whom you have something in common. Be open to letting these new people into your life.

- Use your alone time to get deeper into yourself and learn more about who you are. Think of time alone as an opportunity to develop self-reliance and to learn to take care of your own emotional needs. You can grow in important ways during time alone, being creative and enjoying activities that are meaningful. You may cherish the feelings of awe, love, peace, joy, and tenderness during time spent by yourself.

8

You Can Be Alone but Not Lonely

People with poor self-image find themselves in a spirit of loneliness. They fear they can never be known and loved. They hope there is one person in the world who will truly know them and love them anyway. They believe, "there is someone who will love me perfectly—without conditions or reservations and for all time. Then I will be happy."

Leave me alone. Why don't you leave me alone? I want to be alone for a while. How many times do we hear comments like these from young and old alike who prefer not to be interrupted by anyone or anything? The concept of aloneness implies isolation from others but does not necessarily mean unhappiness. There are times when each of us would prefer to be alone for whatever personal reasons.

In times of joy or sorrow, however, when all friends seem to disappear and the day goes by uneventfully, loneliness generates unhappiness. There is a difference between wanting to be alone and feeling lonely. Many people mistakenly believe that the two words, *alone* and *lonely*, refer to the same condition. The objective of this chapter is to define the difference between these two conditions so that we may combat them effectively.

Aloneness vs. Loneliness

In chapter seven there is enough information about the condition of loneliness. It is a depressing state of mind that no human being desires yet many people experience. It is a feeling of emptiness, an attitude of inability to face the world alone. In short, some people seek babysitters for themselves, anyone willing to take them by the hand and lead them into greener pastures of enjoyment and fulfillment. They look for someone to accept, amuse, comfort, divert, distract, provide solutions, support, and reassure them so that they will not become responsible for or aware of their contribution to their loneliness. Unable to find even one person to make them the center of attention, they plunge into a deeper and abiding feeling of loneliness. Such individuals usually find it difficult to establish any lasting relationship because they are so passive, nonproductive, and shallow in their lives that others find them boring companions. They continually convey negativity by describing all the wrongs that have happened in their life or complain about the injustices of life and pay little or no attention to the concerns of others. Eventually they find themselves avoided or rejected. *Nobody cares. People are aloof and self-absorbed,* they say, and they walk away, wallowing in self-pity, attributing their condition to others. Lonely people have not learned how to apply themselves in a productive manner.

As hard as it may sound, lonely people have to realize their deeper needs—what makes them so lonely—and to understand the reality that there are few rescuers out there to remove their loneliness. They need to retrain themselves to take other initiatives, to find an activity that stirs their curiosity, to build, to make, to discover, to explore, and to improvise something of interest in the world around them.

Aloneness is incomparably different from loneliness. It is a return to one's own self. The teacher of teachers, Jesus Christ, who spent three years with his people, healing their infirmities and daily teaching them a new way of life, gives a number of examples of being alone. He withdrew from the crowds that followed him and sought to be alone. Periodically, we too need time alone to appreciate God's presence in our life, to discover the riches within, to hear the voice of our soul reminding us that we are God's special creation. In addition to realizing that each one of us is a unique creature in this world, we must also accept that at times we need to be alone. While we are born among people, live with people, and die surrounded by people, no one can ever think what we are thinking or feel what are feeling. Whether we are surrounded by a group of relatives, friends, or hundreds of people, our authentic self is alone. The experience of being alone is either liberating or enslaving, depending upon what we choose to do with it. We have a choice, however, to make it a liberating experience that can be beneficial to us emotionally, physically, and spiritually.

When the world around us seems to have grown cold and meaningless, and when life becomes too demanding and societal expectations increase, our inner self desires a state of peace and tranquility. We want to be alone. It is a time when we no longer feel lonely; we are alone with ourselves. It is a time of dialogue with our self, a personal time for self-inventory and self-evaluation.

In a state of aloneness we are in this world but not of this world. We study each moment and understand life under a different light. When people are alone they have a chance to examine the real nature of their existence, the truth about their thoughts and feelings. They become aware of the emptiness within themselves and discover that what really matters is taking a new direction, a less-traveled path they have not taken before.

Aloneness, then, is a fullness of spirit, a state of grace, and knows no feeling of want, poverty, or discomfort. On one hand, loneliness is the empty world of seeking external stimulation or fulfillment. It is the feeling of children who get lost in a crowd and are unable to find their parents; they become terrified and do not know what to do. On the other hand, aloneness is complete; it is a warm feeling that a child experiences in the safety of the arms of a loving mother.

For anyone who wants to experience a state of aloneness, the first step is to eliminate the distractions, to simplify life. Understandably, total withdrawal from our environment is not possible. We cannot ignore our responsibilities. We cannot permanently inhabit a private room. We cannot be monastic in the midst of a family setting. The answer is neither in the renunciation of the world nor in total immersion in it. We need a balance or an alternating rhythm between these two extremes, between aloneness and loneliness. When we take time out to be alone, we will learn something to carry back into our worldly life.

A second step may be concerned with neurotic attachment to things. Look around your house or your basement or your garage or your office and see how many gadgets you have accumulated over the years. At one time or another you bought these items—maybe you used them, maybe not—and now they are lying around collecting dust. Ask yourself: *Do these objects facilitate or hinder my life?* Most of these items are no longer important, but you hold on to them in the hope that some day they may be of value. Dealing with clutter consumes much of our time and energy.

In the process of putting our house in order, removing or getting rid of the clutter, we gain an idea of how we can cleanse our minds. Material possessions that we can touch and move are easily appropriated or discarded.

This technique can be applied on the emotional level. We can take a parallel step to rid ourselves of dishonesty, hostility, hypocrisy, jealousy, and the desire to impress others. What a relief this can be when we unclutter our minds, letting go of wrong values and old grudges, the baggage we carry.

※ ※ ※

When our interaction with others is superficial or lacks sincerity, our life becomes emotionally exhausting. This was the case of Frances, a forty-four year old executive in a big firm in New York City who came to my office for counseling seven years ago. Highly respected and financially well-rewarded by her company, she could afford designer clothing and was able to invest a couple of hours weekly luxuriating in a spa. Although her wealthy husband showered her with a variety of expensive jewelry, vacations in resorts, and travel overseas, she had experienced a sense of loneliness in recent years. She wanted to understand its meaning. She told me she was treated as a celebrity at work, but in the evening when she came home, the reception by her husband was lukewarm. *At night, I sit in my living room and keep staring at my husband, hoping for intimate conversation. But he shows no interest in what I have to say or how I feel. He is usually involved in reading the* Wall Street Journal.

Shifting position gently on the chair, she said, "He's so emotionally detached and preoccupied that he is totally oblivious to the swirling thoughts in my mind." She took a couple of deep breaths, sighed, and informed me that she had a strange feeling that this man to whom she had been married for twenty-four years, the man to whom she had given two beautiful daughters, did not even know her. "At times I see him as a total stranger sitting there in my living room which I've worked hard to decorate and make beautiful. He doesn't care about me. I've come to the realization for the first time that this man would never, ever know my private inner thoughts, feelings, and needs."

It was evident that the feeling Frances experienced at that moment was quite disturbing, and she did not know exactly what to do about it other than to seek professional help. In her first four counseling sessions, she felt frustrated about her situation and thought that she might be better off getting a divorce and living on her own. "Maybe I'll find someone who will appreciate me. I have a good job, feel appreciated at work, and make enough money to have a more rewarding life."

Her counseling continued, and by the seventh session she became aware of the basic truth about what it means to be a human being, and a successful and self-reliant woman in our times. She learned to see the reality of her fundamental loneliness from an entirely different perspective. Since her husband could never think or feel what exactly she was thinking and feeling—no human being could—she needed to stop expecting him to understand her and be *one with her emotionally* all the time. Gradually, she realized that her expectation, as desirable as it was, was unrealistic.

Frances began to feel better when she realized that her husband was also lonely; she was able to relieve herself of the burden of always trying to be connected with him. He was entitled to his own thoughts and feelings, and she did not have to rescue him from his loneliness. Equipped with this insight, she stopped torturing herself with the idea that her husband had to think or feel as she did. She was able to be in total charge of her thoughts and feelings and eliminate her wasteful expectations for her husband—and stop bothering him, too.

It did not take long for Frances to experience a newness of life; she felt like a new woman. Her mind was free from the senseless attempt to expect her husband to join in her own unique thoughts and feelings.

When our expectations of others, especially a significant other, are too high, Frances's experience proves to be a great lesson. She could have turned her loneliness into disaster, as many people do, by seeing herself as a prisoner of her human condition and believing that no one would ever understand her. At the start of counseling, she had done a lot of complaining that her husband did not understand her. *I'm like a stranger to him... He ignores me... I wonder if he ever loved me.* A litany of such complaints would have made her situation hopeless, but she took a deeper look into herself. She realized the futility of trying to get her spouse or anyone to be with her internally. She could share many things of their life together and could get closer with each other, of course, but the truth of their situation is that they could only know each other partially—and that applies in every relationship. There is no way that one individual could possibly know or understand the total truth about another individual. Omnipotence is only God's prerogative. The best we can do is to accept the other, to respect his or her being as we accept ourselves and (within reason) to interact with others honestly. All of us are entitled to be in charge of our private feelings and reserve the right as to what to share and what to keep in our inner sanctum.

Periodically, Frances recalls those moments in her living room as the most important in her life, because not only did they get her into counseling and give her the freedom to halt her effort to have her husband feeling what she was feeling. They also gave her the strength to be herself in a more powerful and positive way. We gain greater strength and more clarity of mind when we stop trying to get everyone else to feel what we are feeling and stand up for what we believe. Frances still believes that no human being is entirely an island who can function as an antisocial hermit, but she now knows, by virtue of having experienced it, that internally we are islands unique unto ourselves. It is our choice whether to come to grips with this idea, which will help us build bridges to others, rather than erecting barriers by being upset when we see that others are not like us.

This new direction affords us a vision, hope, and excitement. Aloneness is the self-reliant, independent inner life when we have finally shut our ears to the competing and compelling voices of external authorities. When we let go of our own desire to impress, control, or compete, the voice of our inner self will be clear. As we let go of our need for personal recognition and other remnants of our childhood needs, the new direction will emerge in front of us. A whole new world will open inside us. Everything around us—our thoughts, feelings, and actions—will come to life with a nature of their own. Our vision will be clear, and we will accept things as they are, without a desire to distort, improve, modify, or change the outside world at all.

Many theorists claim that loneliness lies at the heart of mental illness. We are aware that it causes isolation and pain. In making a transition from loneliness to aloneness, however, we can harvest many benefits. Too many people are so afraid of being alone that they never allow themselves to experience it. If family, friends, or movie theaters are not available, there is still an iPod or TV or the Internet to fill the void. When we plan time out to be alone, our soul can breathe and blossom, and our mind will rest and come up with some new thoughts, better feelings, and healthier life.

The Answer to Loneliness

Loneliness is a painful emotion. It is a feeling that most of us experience from time to time and try to diffuse with some activity. We feel physically tired or emotionally fatigued, unmotivated, or depressed. When loneliness continues to be an issue, it can be damaging to our self-image and lifestyle. Sometimes it can affect us physically. If we do not deal with loneliness, other attitudes may develop. Lonely people tend to feel unworthy, unloved, unfit, undesired, and they build a fence around themselves, closing themselves in and closing others out. Their thoughts tell them: *Nobody loves me or cares how I feel.* In their search for relief from loneliness, they resort to destructive habits. Some people seek the answer in drinking or drugging or smoking, or having affairs, or indulging in lust or pornography. What appears as temporary escape undermines peace of mind and self-esteem, produces no results, leads to depression, and in some situations leads to suicide.

Lonely people are disconnected from their authentic self, from their significant other, and from God. Their deeper self—their soul—is suffering. They may deny that they are lonely: *Oh well, that's what life is all about.* They may blame circumstances, other things, or other people for their loneliness. In essence, though, they know their current condition is harmful, and yet they continue against any hope to seek the answer in the wrong places and wasteful ways.

The only one secure answer to loneliness is the awareness that we are good people in the eyes of God. Believing and becoming conscious that we are children of God, our loving Father, can bring about the greatest comfort to our hearts. This awareness becomes real as we connect with God through a relationship with Jesus Christ. *Relationship* means being connected meaningfully with someone. To describe a relationship *with Jesus* implies that we believe in Him as our Savior and Redeemer. God in Jesus accepts us, forgives us, loves us unconditionally, and wants us to be happy. His infinite love is focused on each one of us, even if our response is different, depending on our disposition. Deep down our hearts yearn to be loved and to love.

The presence of Jesus cannot be grasped by human intelligence; with Jesus, it is an issue of faith and trust, an affair of the heart. Human relationships are fragile, and sometimes people we love let us down, in which case we feel betrayed, misunderstood or ignored. But our relationship with Jesus is the strongest; it is one that can be trusted. He is our best friend, our caring brother, and our wise mentor. He is closest to those who believe in Him and are faithful.

Jesus wants us to love and trust Him with our whole heart. He loves us and wants us to love one another. He said, *Love one another as I have loved you.* In Matthew 22:37–40, Jesus let us know that *loving God* and *loving others* are two of the greatest commandments. Spiritual growth becomes evident as we come closer to Jesus through prayer and living a godly life. This is not to say that we would not face negative emotions at times, but the key is to deal with them as they surface.

Love is a positive and creative energy that puts us in good standing with our Creator. Since God knows us better than we know ourselves, He also knows our pace and understands that it takes time for us to connect with Him genuinely. Building intimacy with Jesus may be a slow process. As we trust Jesus to guide us through the Holy Spirit, our intimacy with Him builds. We feel more and more comfortable in this Great Adventure we call life. It continues from day to day. All we need to do is to pause for a second and say, *Lord, thank you for another day.* "This is the day that the Lord has made *for me.* I shall rejoice and be glad in it" (See Psalm 118:24).

Trusting that Jesus is mindful of our needs is crucial to building intimacy with Him. His presence becomes our reality. When we trust that He will carry us through this day, through difficult times, we are rewarded with inner strength and conviction that He is ever present in our life. Listen to the voice of David:

> *To you, O Lord, I lift up my soul. O my God, it is you I trust… Turn to me and be gracious to me, for I am lonely and afflicted. Relieve the trouble of my heart, and bring me out of my distress. Consider my affliction and my trouble and forgive all my sins.* (Ps 25)

✳ ✳ ✳

"I don't believe there is a God," said Steve, my brother-in-law. "It's the fear of death that caused people to invent God."

"Steve, if that's what you believe," I said, "let me ask a few questions. Your parents caused your birth, but who gave life to your conception in your mother's womb? You were born with a perfectly functioning body, you had no physical defects or adverse environmental conditions, and your body has tried to protect you for many years. Who was that mastermind that created you?"

Steve's smile turned into a grimace of disbelief.

"As you inhale air, you don't tell your lungs how to breathe or how to take in oxygen and exhale carbon dioxide. You don't tell your eyes to blink, to create tears so they don't get irritated. When you eat every day, you don't tell your stomach how to digest your food. You don't train your veins to carry blood to your heart at a certain rate or direct your arteries to carry blood back . Now, tell me who makes all those parts of your body work in such harmony and always for your benefit? Your mother didn't teach your heart how to beat or your brain to think."

Feeling uncomfortable and shifting positions in his chair, Steve giggled nervously. "Well, nature does all that for all of us. It doesn't mean that there is a God."

The purpose of my discussion was not to persuade my brother-in-law to follow what I believe. So I brought our dialogue to a close by saying: "Steve, I'm going to pray for you. But I have a prayer that you could use. It could prove of benefit."

"A prayer?" He smiled.

"Yes, a prayer."

"But I never pray."

"Try this one for a while," I said. "O God, I do not know if you exist, but if you do, help me to find you. Amen."

There are many people like Steve, good people who call themselves agnostics, unbelievers, atheists, and so forth. My purpose is not to convert anyone to my faith. God gave free will to all, and people have choices. When we do not believe or trust God, we are left to our own devices, which are usually not very effective. Trust is not something you and I can test, but it can be developed. We have a choice either to trust or not.

Think of Peter, who knew Jesus. He witnessed His miracles and lived with Him for three years. When he saw

Jesus walking on water, he said: *Lord, if it is You, command me to come to You on the water.* Jesus said, *Come.* So Peter got out of the boat and started walking on the water toward Jesus. But when he noticed the strong wind, he became frightened, and beginning to sink, he cried out, *Lord, save me!* Jesus immediately reached out his hand and caught him, saying to him, *You of little faith, why did you doubt?*

When Peter put his trust in Jesus and listened to his command *Come*, he was able to walk on water. But the moment he engaged his mind to test his trust, he began to sink. It is evident that we either have to trust and listen to Jesus' command, or not trust. This is our challenge. There are times in our lives that even during our prayer or church attendance, a doubt may surface. As long as we do not wallow in doubt, the divine hand will reach out and relieve us.

We would not expect to develop an intimate relationship with another person if we did not trust him or her, would we? Why should it be any different with God? One of the best ways we can trust and listen to God is through his Word, the Bible. If you have a Bible, start reading it, and you will find it easy to understand and apply your reading to your day-to-day life. Pick up a Bible story and meditate on it. Make it personal and see how it applies to you. What is God telling you? The more you read the Bible, the better you know the mind of God. Jesus reveals his ways and his Father's will through this holy book. Many people who read the New Testament for the first time discover that God is much kinder, more gentle, loving, and compassionate than they thought. But you need to be alone to calm your mind and relax your body to absorb what you are reading. Time alone is vital to sense Christ's presence in your life. If you expect visions to see the face of Jesus or to hear His voice, you'll be disappointed. But if you insist upon seeing His face, I suggest you look into the face of a smiling baby; it is completely vulnerable and depends on its parents as we depend on God. Think of teenagers in search of certain freedoms, think of the young men and women who seek to find their place in life, the middle-aged persons who are still looking for fulfillment in their lives, the ill who fight to survive, the prisoners, and the persecuted who await their liberty. There you find Jesus, incarnated in each one. The experience of seeing Jesus in others is the result of openness to the power of God's spirit working in and through all people. It is the reorientation of one's view from the lofty and mighty to the simple and humble, even to the most despised and neglected among us.

The Apostle John suggests that we should try to sense Jesus within us, to let Him live His life through us, and give Him the whole of our being to become His instruments, to be a continuation of His humanity. An intimate relationship is a one-to-one relationship with no distractions. To build intimacy with Jesus Christ, you must spend time alone with Him. You have to want it enough to stop all the noise and focus your life on Him.

The Burning Candle: A Personal Story

I will indulge to share with you a recent experience when I sought solitude to be alone with Jesus, with no distractions or noise, The third week of September in the year 2008, I was visiting Samos, a Greek island, a true diamond of the Aegean Sea. At the top of an afforested hill is a glorious chapel dedicated to St. Fanourios, a saint who uncovers lost items and reveals direction in life. One evening I entered this sacred chapel, lit a candle, and sat for a few moments in prayer and meditation. As I began to pray, suddenly my spirit felt dejected. Wearied and oppressed by my sense of loneliness, I questioned the nature of my thoughts: preoccupation with my current life, getting older, health issues, and fear of death. That kind of thinking makes us vulnerable to the evil that is capable of transforming us into dishonest or conniving persons, even when we are honest and good by nature.

Where is your faith and trust in God? I asked myself. The answer gradually surfaced in my mind: *God is ever-present in your life. He is with you now.* It was a peak time of solitude in my life, an awesome time that I did not expect. It was a time I shall cherish for the rest of my life.

As evening approached, the chapel became darker, but the lighted candle provided abundant light for me to appreciate the beauty of my surroundings. Being alone and away from external sounds and distractions, I felt lighter, as if all my worries had been lifted from my shoulders. Silently, my mind allowed me to think of my life, to think about who I really was. In silence, peacefully I observed how my mind and feelings function. It became evident that a thought always surfaces first, and then follows the feeling. Not all the thoughts that arose from my mind were positive, and not all feelings were pleasant. Some were negative thoughts that precipitated emotions of anger, anxiety, fear, insecurity, or resentment. Here I was in a holy place, a hospitable home, a refuge for those persecuted by inner and outer enemies. Fixing my eyes on the candle, I could see beyond it a Byzantine icon of Christ, strikingly depicting His divinity. I became conscious that I had inner enemies, nagging feelings over sins I had committed. A glance into my past made me aware that my conscience sought relief from guilt. The face of Christ reflected acceptance, compassion, forgiveness, and love. In my mind I could hear His gentle voice: *The one who comes to Me, I will certainly not cast out. For I have come down from heaven.*

It was time for me to move deeper into myself, to uncover and combat my enemies. I tore a page from a notebook I carry in my pocket and wrote down my sins—wrong and unwitting errors I had committed in my life since the age of five until the present. The list was long and painful. Admitting my past evoked feelings of guilt. All of a sudden my past became vividly present. Once more I went over my list to assure myself I had not forgotten anything. Slowly I stood up, took my list, and held it over the candle. The flame instantly turned the list to ashes. Sighs and tears escaped me, and I felt lighter. God's grace and mercy soothed my soul. I had allowed my inner being to admit honestly the wrongs of my past. There was no need to repress aspects of my life of which I no longer approved. As I surrendered to God's mercy all of my past life that caused my guilt feelings, I felt new energy surfacing in my being. Comforting words from John Chrysostom, a father of the Early Church, came to mind: *When sparks of fire fall into the ocean, does the ocean catch on fire? Of course not! Our sins are like sparks; the ocean is like the mercy of God. The mercy and love of God extinguish our sins.* Trusting in God's abundant love, I believed God had forgiven me. The power of forgiveness is one of the most powerful spiritual tools and virtues. Forgiveness is one of the attributes of God's love. Think of where the world would be if we could forgive.

Now my challenge became evident: I must learn to forgive myself for my imperfections, I must learn to forgive others, and I must accept the world and other people for what they are. This was a breakthrough in my life. I felt happier, healthier, and more loving.

As I meditated on events in Christ's life—He forgave sins and healed the sick—I realized that a catharsis of negative emotions could be a positive experience in that it represents an expression of energy. Energy can create change. If I did not have some negative emotions, I could not have a passion for life. Passion makes us come alive. I thought of my wife Pat, and although she was back home in New Jersey, five thousand miles away, I felt intimately close to her. How I wished she were sitting next to me at that moment. I thanked God that after three more days I would be at home again near her. *I am a fortunate man,* I thought, *to love and to be loved by my wife. Having her in my life, I feel fulfilled.* During three decades we both managed to convert our initial romance into enduring love. The task ahead of us was to live life with vigor, joy, and gratitude, to remain committed to our marriage and to being lifetime friends.

The candle burned slowly and became shorter, but its glowing flame danced gracefully in the dark and sent profound messages to my heart. I thought of myself as being the candle; my lifetime on this earth was gradually getting shorter. How did I reach the great age of 82? Many changes have taken place within me—my biochemistry, my physical appearance, and my perceptions of life. I realize that I have gone from fifty years to sixty, to seventy, and to eighty without paying much attention to what was happening. The lighted candle represented the light that I could bring into the world. The candle, after offering its light, will eventually die. Like the candle, some day I too will die. But that is God's territory. He will decide when to call me to my heavenly home.

Meanwhile, I'm happy to see myself as another imperfect human being and in need of God's mercy even to the very end of my life. I'm aware of my destiny and am at peace with it. My body is aging; bones are aching, hair is thinning, and I have difficulty getting a restful sleep at night. While these are normal symptoms of an elderly citizen, my life does not have to follow such a pattern. I shall keep my candle lit as long as I can; I'll eat healthy foods, exercise faithfully, and avoid toxic relationships that cause stress. I'll continue reading instructive material and keep writing self-help books to share with others the lessons I have learned and am still learning day by day.

Thoughts You May Consider

- If you feel that something is missing in your life, that something has escaped you and is lost, do not look outside to find the answer. It is time to take a journey into yourself to explore the core of your being and its needs. This journey is not a lonely one, although you have to take it alone.
- In your journey alone, your life's story may not be pleasant, sweet, and harmonious, as some contrived stories are. Yet it is *your story*, and that is important. How you decide to rewrite it is your business. Alone, you may discover some good qualities in yourself. Accept them and cherish them.
- Choose to be alone some regular time each day. Ten or twenty minutes can replenish your energy and refine your thoughts. During this time you may be in touch with the true essence of your life and how you perceive it. This is a time in which you experience your totality as a human being.
- You don't have to wait until you get to heaven to know God better. He wants to give all of Himself to you right

here, right now. Intimacy with Jesus is the highest good. It is constructive and life-enhancing, a most thrilling adventure that provides lasting joy.

- Reading the Bible and reflecting on events in the life of Jesus is time spent alone with Him. Meditate on any one of the encounters of Jesus with His people and envision yourself being there today. See how that experience applies to you. The Holy Spirit will direct your reading and your thoughts, and He will give you the insights He wants you to have.

9

Solitude: Choosing to Be Alone

Solitude provides a unique experience in which our nature is nurtured. In solitude the mind gains strength and learns to lean upon itself. Back in the world it seeks or tolerates a few unreliable supports—the feigned compassions of one, the flattery of a second, the civilities of a third, the friendship of a fourth or the pseudo-amenities of the fifth. Solitude has one disadvantage, however—excessive solitude can evoke hubris.

Loneliness and *solitude* both imply being alone. The difference is that solitude is a choice people make. Loneliness, on the other hand, is marked by a sense of isolation and emotional detachment. When you experience loneliness, you feel that something is missing. It is possible to be with people and still feel lonely—and this is, perhaps, the most difficult form of loneliness.

Solitude is a state of being alone without being lonely, and it can lead to self-awareness. It is a positive and constructive state of engagement with yourself. It is a desirable state of being alone, during which time you provide yourself with your own company and have time to think, time to feel, and time to make worthwhile plans. From the outside, solitude and loneliness look alike. Both are characterized by solitariness. But all resemblance ends at the surface. Solitude is a time that may be used for reflection, inner searching, growth, or enjoyment. Praying, thinking, serious reading, and creating—all require solitude.

Jesus Christ sought solitude. Tired and weary after a long day among throngs of people, teaching them a new way of life, loving and forgiving sinners, healing the afflicted, and resurrecting the dead, He pulled away to be alone. His human nature needed rest, time alone, and quiet time with his Father.

All of us need time alone to relax, to enjoy a hobby, to reflect on our lives. Solitude is the time to pull our individual selves together, to plan, to organize, to create, to meditate— and for believers, it is a time to connect with their Creator in prayer and worship. Short-term solitude is often valued as a time when you may work, think, or rest without being distracted. It may be desired for privacy. Meaningful solitude can be a powerful experience and a necessary tonic in today's speed-oriented and stress-inducing society. People who pursue solitude are refreshed and revitalized, and are able to connect in a meaningful way with others. *Time-out* has been heralded as a coping strategy, a time to pull back and debrief. Time-out, however, suggests that in the theater of life, relating and being stimulated are the important issues, and *time-alone* is merely the intermission. In truth, each profoundly enriches the other. So, let's rediscover the joys of solitude.

Today, people caught in a struggle to produce work at the rate expected by society do not always consider the lack of alone moments for themselves. When they realize the necessity of having alone time, they may decide to take control of their professional life by turning down promotions, shifting careers, or changing to a less pressured field. In our fast-paced, high tech times, we need our periods of solitude. Being alone gives us the power to regulate and adjust our lives. It can give us fortitude and the ability to satisfy our own needs. Solitude is a restorer of energy. It gives us time to explore and regain perspective of our inner self. Solitude is the necessary counterpoint to intimacy; it is what allows us to have a self-worth to share. It renews us for the challenges of life. It allows us to reach a position of being in charge of our own lives, rather than having our years run by external schedules and demands.

The concept of solitude can differ from person to person. Some people may seek physical seclusion to remove distractions and make it easier to concentrate, reflect, or meditate. Others develop a certain capacity to become less sensitive to distractions and more capable of maintaining mindfulness and staying inwardly absorbed and focused. Long-term solitude, however, can be undesirable, causing loneliness or depression, or an inability to establish relationships, so we must be careful. For many people, though, solitude is not an escape from life—it is food for the soul. For others, particularly monks and nuns, solitude is regarded as a means of spiritual growth and purification. In religious terminology, solitude means the experience of feeling the presence of God. Monastics have much godly wisdom to convey to us about the need for time alone and the need to detach from worldly affairs. Both *monastery* and *monk* stem from the same Greek word, *monos*, meaning *alone*. The word *convent* comes from the Latin *convenire*, which means *to meet together.* The origins of these two words, *monastery* and *convent*, linguistically combine the two basic human needs: the need to be alone and the need to be together. God did not create us to be alone. In Genesis, when God created man, He says: *It is not good for man to be alone; I will make him a helper comparable to him* (Gen 1:18). God created human beings with fellowship in mind. That means He wants us to interact with other people in a spirit of cooperation and love.

Have you ever wondered what often blocks the potential for a good relationship? Why is it that a talented person hampers her own creativity? What prevents our peace of mind? One surprising answer in this age of alienation is a lack of solitude. We live in a society that worships independence, speed, and over-stimulation. Small and large nations, cities, and towns around the world have revolutionized social relationships. Computers, contemporary technology, iPods, Facebook, and cell phones extend the domain of our lives into every part of the world. Religion hardly provides a place for quiet retreat and inspiration. Some churches, in an effort to attract more members, have become entertainment centers and function like country clubs. We are terminally out of touch with the essence of life. The awareness of the need for genuine and constructive solitude has become utterly lost, and, in the process, we have lost our souls. We feel overloaded, and we overreact to minor annoyances; we feel as if we can never catch up.

The need for solitude is essential to human peace and survival. Mother Nature gives time to be totally detached from involvements of high priority: sleep is nature's way of ensuring solitude. Personally, I experience enormous benefits from time alone. I either take a long walk alone or go swimming. During this time, I have a chance to think about different aspects of life or ideas I can incorporate in a book I am writing. At certain times when I chose to seek solitude, I experience a profound feeling of gratitude to God for His abundant blessings in my life.

I have known a number of people who periodically take time out to be alone. They have shared with me the enormous benefits of solitude. It actually strengthens their relationships with others and makes them more productive in their work. A young man who works for a school system as a guidance counselor confided in me that in spending some time totally alone, he truly feels more lovable and loved by his wife. In his words: *Intimacy between us is remarkable, for each one knows how to please the other. Yet we do not go to bed or wake up at the same time, and in the morning we have breakfast, sip our coffee, and read the paper. Then we take separate paths. Each one spends an hour or more alone. We need those solitary hours, and as we treasure our time alone, we return to each other with greater yearning.* Such a practice seems to be the essence of their intimacy.

When listening to patients talk about their spouses, lovers, family, or friends, I am struck by their expressions of gratitude when they take *time off* to engage in independent pursuits. Like prisoners who are granted parole, they feel that their freedom is a gracious gift. Both the need to be alone and the need to engage others are essential to human happiness and survival. Solitude restores body and mind. It is a great protector of the self and the human spirit. Solitude allows us to reflect and sort things out. It is not necessarily a way to escape from bonding, for often we find our way back and forge stronger commitments. Solitude is an important route to creativity.

Experience and research on creative and talented people suggest that creativity requires solitude. The artist in each of us must risk some disconnection; forging a happy and worthwhile life—and navigating through that life fully and gracefully—is itself a creative act. Kahlil Gibran writes, *Let there be spaces in your togetherness.* This makes sense for husbands and wives who truly love each other. Even these partners find it refreshing to have a little personal time. Instead of complaining, *I have problems with you. You demand a lot of my time,* it would be more appropriate to say, *I need to be alone for a while.*

In solitude, taking time to be in contact with our inner selves, struggles occur that are hard to determine. Inner battles are fought that seldom become inspirational illustrations for books. God, who probes our deepest thoughts during protracted segments of solitude, opens our eyes to things that need attention. It is here that He makes us aware of those things we try to hide from others.

Most of us resist more intensive soul-searching because it seems too severe. Contemplation seems to be the preferred mode for achieving spiritual peace, which is why journeys on the way to truth or salvation are undertaken alone. Religious pilgrimages, in the traditional sense, still occur today, but they are briefer than they were in olden days; we even see in people's recreational walks and runs attempts to escape the hectic pace of life and rid the mind of excess.

For religion to have its greatest appeal, it must allow time for solitude. The Book of Genesis lays this foundation. Within the creation story, God establishes Saturday, the Shabbat, as a day of rest, set aside from all others. The Shabbat was a time to contemplate one's life and study the scriptures. We can do the same, whether we take a day of rest or an hour of quiet prayer or even just a few minutes of meditation.

Romantic love and a stable relationship were once assumed to be antithetical to each other. Now, a recent study on couples suggests, the two are imagined to exist in harmony. Partners are supposed to be able to switch from lawn mowing and diaper changing to torrid sex at the drop of a hat and from long hours at work to sweet moments in the sun. The demand on couples to be all things to each other is stressful. Can all this be accomplished without one of the partners calling for a time-out? Obviously not, for it seems that as the push for greater and greater intimacy between people grows, the percentage of couples seeking separation and divorce rises.

Thoughts You May Consider

- As the world spins faster and faster—or maybe it just seems to do so since emails can travel around the world in a fraction of a second—we mortals need a variety of ways to cope with the resulting pressures. Taking a long walk in the park, sitting under a tree and meditating, or finding a quiet place to relax and read a favorite book can be most rewarding.

- Solitude suggests peacefulness stemming from a state of inner richness. It is a means of enjoying the quiet and the sustenance it brings. It is something to cultivate. Solitude is refreshing, an opportunity to renew ourselves. In other words, it replenishes our potential.

- Make solitude part of the social norm. Then uplift it from its lowly place on the mental health shelf. The relief provided by solitude, reverie, contemplation, aloneness, and private times is inestimable. Remember, love is not all there is to psychic wellbeing; work and creativity also sustain this health, and so does solitude.

- Many idealized lovers or spouses become ordinary human beings. With the recognition of this reality, a restlessness born from too little time alone also becomes apparent. Gradually each partner has to return to his or her individual concerns in life. Couples who successfully handle this transition usually do so through a renegotiation of the amount and condition of time spent together.

- When a spouse says *I need space,* the other may interpret that as rejection. Significant changes occur when a man and a woman feel attracted to each other.

Initially, they explore each other's likes and dislikes. When things become more serious, important questions are raised: *Where do you want to live? Do you want children? Do you like to be alone?* This kind of dialogue enables people to discuss their own needs without unnecessary quarrels.

10

No Parent Is Perfect

Children will never know the quality of love of their parents until they become parents themselves. As parents bend over the cradle of their own children, eventually they realize the mystery and sacredness of a mother's and a father's love. In later years as children grow, become adults, and leave home, parents experience certain mixed feelings—sadness to see them leave, joy to see them established and happy.

If you were ever abandoned or rejected by your mother or father, try to understand that the problem was not with you but with them. It so happens that many parents who abandon or reject their children were themselves rejected, but they never found a way or took the time to work out their own difficulties. They passed their difficulties on to you. Perhaps the rejection occurred because your parents were not ready to be parents—maybe they were immature. Most married couples are biologically able to conceive and give birth to a child, but that is the easiest part. Living with the child, loving the child, and meeting the child's needs does not come naturally. Your parents may have had a deficiency in their capacity or desire to be loving and caring. Parenting takes depth of character, dedication, maturity, patience, sensitivity, and wisdom. Perhaps these were absent in your early years, as was the case for many of us. The title of this chapter reminds us that *no parent is perfect.*

As we explore human relationships, it is fascinating to notice the extent to which parents determine the potential of an individual. Many specialists estimate that, in a lifetime, most people use about one-fifth of their actual abilities. How fantastic it would be if we made full use of these inherent talents and intelligence! It would make a huge difference to the population if parents used their own potential to be good parents and be effectively creative in relationships. Good and cooperative parenting protects growing children from feeling abandoned or emotionally lonely.

It has always been easy to see what went wrong with the family across the street, or how other men or women might have improved their lot. Life would be easier if significant people in our life—parents, spouses, children, friends, and others—would change, so that we would not have to change. How realistic is that expectation?

As we focus on the father figure, we see him as a desired model for a little boy to imitate. It is usually the first male that any baby boy meets, and the one from whom he learns what it means to be a man. Their relationship is most important, especially for the formation of the son's character. If the father shows genuine love and interest in his son, the son develops an inner desire to emulate his father. *I want to be like you, Dad!* In some situations, this desire may last a lifetime. There is nothing wrong with the idea *like father, like son*, unless the growing boy fails to develop his own identity as a separate individual. Correspondingly, these dynamics apply to a girl who interacts with her mother. There is nothing wrong when initially a girl imitates her mother. *I want to be like you, Mom.* From her father she learns male behavior patterns.

Many parents fail in this area of modeling appropriate behavior for their children. Parents need a better understanding of circumstances and child development.

Disciplining children by punishing and restricting them is not as effective as persuading them through love and modeling. Today's parents cannot just imitate their father or mother, for the style of parenting in past years is not considered suitable for today's child. There is no doubt, however, that parental attempts to discipline growing children were interwoven with parental concern and love. They did what they could, and they meant well.

There is always a lesson that parents learn but do not recognize until later years when their children become adults. The lesson is that parents exercise tremendous influence upon children when they are young. We need to be careful that our programming is neither negative nor condoning. It may be natural to raise our children as our parents raised us, and if that be the case, then our adult lives will tend to be similar to those of our parents. The hope is that we will take the best attributes from each of our parents, and as we grow older, improve on them to match our emerging present-day personality. If we become parents, we should have a better understanding of parenting than our own parents had.

For healthy emotional growth, the way parents and children interact is crucial and equally critical as they deal with the expectations they hold for each other. Truly, volumes have been written about parent-child interactions and healthy parenting. An easy, perhaps non-threatening way to illustrate these points is to focus on storytelling to provide examples. The externalization of the process of day-to-day family life, as we see in children's stories, helps us see our problems reflected in others; we see how the problems occur and how they can be resolved. For example, a mother tells the story of a baby bird that falls from the nest while its mother is out searching for food. The story serves a unique purpose: it opens the way to verbalize and examine a child's own anxiety about being separated from its mother. The child sees how the baby bird eventually returns safely back in its nest. Likewise, a child will always be protected and safe because parental love is present. A father, on the other hand, may add his perspective to the story. For example, he may introduce the process of how birds come to life. The mother bird sits on the eggs to keep them warm until they hatch. Later, when the mother goes out of the nest to find food, the father bird sits on the eggs to keep them warm and protect them. He opens the way to reassure the child of his protection and the importance of sharing responsibilities at home. The simple expressions of parental love evolve as the child grows and continues to feel the parents' influence.

Through the ages, teachers and sages used parables—stories taken from everyday life—to make a point. It seems that it is easier for any audience to remember a story than an actual message. Yet, as the story is recounted, its meaning surfaces and leaves a lasting lesson.

Parental Influence:
A Lesson from the Movies

A story that had an impact in my life as a father is dramatically illustrated in the film version of Robert Anderson's play, *I Never Sang for My Father*, produced in 1970. The title itself indicates the deeper yearning that children have to connect with their father.

This is a story about the Garrisons, an upper middle-class WASP family that lives in Westchester County, New York. The major theme involves the relationship between father and son. The father, Tom, and mother, Margaret, are in their eighties. The father, at one time a successful businessman and former mayor of the town, has been retired for fifteen years. The mother is in poor health with a deteriorating cardiac condition.

The marriage of Tom and Margaret produced two children. The older daughter, Alice, is estranged from her parents because she married a Jew. She lives with her husband and children in Chicago. Gene, the younger son, is an author who lives in New York City. On a recent visit to California, Gene meets and falls in love with Peggy, a doctor who had been married at one time and is the mother of two children.

The film opens with Gene picking up his parents, on their return to New York from Florida. During the drive from the airport to their home, certain parts of the family life become clear. We notice Tom's pompousness and emotional distance from Margaret. His interest lies in objects, productivity, and material accomplishments.

Margaret is an optimist, emotionally more tuned-in and more relationship-oriented than her husband. She has handled Tom's distance by being emotionally over-invested in her children. Tom is relieved of the job of dealing with his wife's intensity since she is involved in a tight relationship with her children, especially with her son. At times, Tom feels that he is on the outside looking in, and conveniently occupies himself at work.

As the family sits together at dinnertime, Margaret seems subdued, and the son, Gene, in an effort to cheer his parents, wants to tell them about his prize-winning story, but Tom interrupts and tells another heroic story of his own accomplishments in business. At the end of his story, Tom senses the reaction of his listeners. He feels uncomfortable, excuses himself, and withdraws to his study to be alone or to watch cowboy movies. His thoughts of himself are: "I'm only a moneymaking machine. Nobody cares about me anyway." Margaret and son find themselves in the living room, where he plays his latest piano composition for her.

The Garrisons represent a typical dysfunctional family. The father lives in his own world. The mother ends up in a close relationship with her son and thus forges a distant relationship between father and son. Similar situations exist where the parents are emotionally and sometimes physically disconnected. They avoid each other, unable to communicate effectively or have an interesting dialogue, or share aspects of their married life, they make their children the focal point. (To learn more about such marriages, I recommend a book by David Code, *To Raise Happy Kids, Put Your Marriage First*.)

The father talks to his son about his mother, emphasizing the mother's deteriorating health. He transmits his anxiety and inability to deal with her in his son's absence. This is a covert manipulation to prevent his son from going to California and marrying the woman he loves. Their dialogue in the garage scene is revealing.

Father: Where did you say your mother is?
Son: In her garden.
Father: You know, Gene, the strain has been awful.
Son: She looks well.
Father: I know, but you can never tell when she might get another of these damned seizures.
Son: It's rough, I know. *[He puts his arm round his father's shoulder.]*
Father: We got your letters from California...but this girl, this woman you mentioned several times . . .
Son: I'll tell you all about California at dinnertime.

Father: I was in California once many years ago. Beautiful country. But if you go out there, I mean to live, it will kill your mother. You know you're her whole life. Yes, you are. Oh, she's fond of your sister, but you are her life!

It is evident that the father uses the mother's emotional attachment to manipulate the son into abandoning the idea of leaving them. The son is outraged that his father would say such things.

In another scene, we see the mother and son in her room. Admiringly, she looks through the son's new book of short stories. Gene is grateful and thanks her, while the father is downstairs watching a Western. When Gene tells his mother about moving to California, she says with teary eyes, "Your father and I can take care of each other."

Aware of his father's objection to his son's marriage to Peggy and the move to California, the son makes the most loving gesture he has ever made in his life. He says to his father, "I know this is your home that you are used to, but I'd like you to come out to California with me. Dad, it's lovely, and we could find an apartment for you near us." The father replies, "Why don't you all come and live here?" The son calmly explains that Peggy, being a doctor, has a medical practice in California and her children's schools and friends are there.

Once again the father uses guilt and manipulation tactics to convince his son not to go to California. He says, "I'm only saying this for your own good. This is your home. Your family is here. I won't be around long, and then it will be all yours." Facing his son's persistent look, he gives up. Angrily, he shouts, "All right. Go ahead. I can manage. Send me a Christmas card, if you remember. From tonight on, you can consider me dead. I gave you everything. You've had everything—things I never had, you ungrateful bastard."

In his rage the son counterattacks: "What do you want for gratitude? I asked you to come with me. What else to you want? If I lived here for the rest of my life it wouldn't be enough for you. Nothing would be enough. You have resented everything you ever gave me. I'm sorry as hell about your miserable childhood but it does not excuse your behavior and it does not make me love you, and I wanted to love you. You hated your father. I saw what it did to you. I did not want to hate you." As he tries to reach out to his father during a vulnerable moment, the angry father tells him, "go away and leave me alone."

This story strikingly represents what can happen in a family when its members fail to see the potential of good things in each other. On the one hand, the father carried into his own family baggage of bad memories, such as his alcoholic father who abandoned him at the age of ten and his abandoned mother. On the other hand, the mother unable to deal with her husband's emotional distance, so she focused her attention on her son whom she idealized.

Gene, in a heroic effort to keep his parents together, cannot interact man-to-man with his father. He relates well with his mother, but he does not talk to his father. His father, a control freak, thinks he always knows what is the best for his son, and this prevents the son from moving forward to make his own life. When father-son frustration becomes unbearable, both men have a destructive confrontation, leaving the son heavy with guilt and the father to die abandoned.

✳ ✳ ✳

In my practice, I have seen many situations end in a way similar to that of the members of the Garrison family—all suffering from irreparable emotional damage. When mother and father avoid each other physically, drift apart emotionally, engage in a power struggle—*I am right and you are wrong*—and feel emotionally abandoned, communications cease, and they involve themselves with their children's life. The children feel confused and insecure, and they react arrogantly, unable to understand their parents' behavior. As a result, they want to run away and abandon their parents or they resort to acting out their frustrations. Feeling emotionally abandoned, they create additional problems in their lives.

The ancient Greek writers had their own style of dramatizing human tragedies and staging them once a year, for the purpose of letting people see, empathize, and understand what could easily destroy their own lives. According to Aristotle, theater, besides being entertaining, was meant to be educational. As the audience experienced the emotion of tragedy, the participants could be purged, relieved of their inner evil forces, and go through a catharsis. It is interesting to note that the Greek word for actor is *ethopios,* meaning *one who creates and teaches ethics.* Even in our times, dramas and stories drawn from life can teach us lessons that we could use for our own benefit.

Thoughts You May Consider

- Although not perfect, parents are people makers. They shape and form a child's character. In the process of raising children, they are not able to meet all of their children's needs because they have needs of their own. Consequently, some children may feel emotionally deprived. When parents are dissatisfied with their married life, and frequent quarrels occur between them, children feel confused, insecure, and angry.

- Children are temporary guests in a family system. They need to be treated well and wisely by their parents or parenting adults. As Kahlil Gibran says, *We may give them our love but not our thoughts. For they have their own thoughts. We may house their bodies but not their souls, for their souls dwell in the house of tomorrow, which we cannot visit, not even in our dreams.* A holistic approach to children's upbringing is necessary to help them develop all facets of themselves—body, mind, and spirit.

- Some parents unwittingly manipulate their children by guilt. This is reflected in messages such as *I have done so much for you, and look how you treat me! I'm your mother, you know, and you only have one mother. I've worked my fingers to the bone. You had everything and I had nothing. I put a roof over your head and clothes on your back—things I never had, you ungrateful...* When a parent says such words, as Tom, the father of the Garrison family, said to his son Gene, he instills in his son a deep feeling of guilt.

- Constant nagging makes growing children listen to voices outside their heads instead of inside. It hinders the need to develop initiative, self-esteem, self-control, or self-discipline because they are used to hearing external voices criticizing or giving them direction. Such children are more susceptible to external influences and pressures, and they lack an identity of their own. Emotionally, they feel abandoned.

11

Abandoned Parents

When a son or a daughter leaves home to establish a new life of their own, the relationship between the left behind parents is significantly affected.

Throughout this book, we've been focusing on the abandoned child. We should pause briefly, however, to note that there are times when matters go in the other direction: Some parents themselves feel abandoned, ignored, or rejected by their children. Although as mature adults they are able to combat feelings of abandonment or rejection and face reality, their minds linger on the Fifth Commandment, "Honor your father and your mother," and they feel entitled to their children's respect and love. Many parents at some point in their lives go through this feeling of abandonment; it can actually prove to be beneficial when the relationship is restored and reconciliation takes place.

A father came to my office for a brief consultation. Being a medical doctor who provided healing for his patients, he had realized that he needed healing himself. For the last three years his personal life had been in turmoil. Steve, his only son for whom he had noble dreams and had spent thousands dollars for his education, refused to have any contact with him. When he sent him a sizeable check for his 35th birthday, Steve sent it back with a nasty note: "I don't need your money, I don't need you. You were never a father to me."

As he spoke about his son's rejection, deep hurt was reflected in his eyes. Silence and a prolonged sigh held back his tears. I wanted to tell this father, *who ever promised us that our children were supposed to make parents happy?*, but instead, I asked for his son's telephone number so I could call him. *Maybe I could act as a mediator to bring about reconciliation,* I thought.

I did call his son, but he didn't seem to want to talk to a psychologist.

"Steve, I saw your father and he looks depressed," I said. "Can you tell me what's going on?"

"I don't care if he's depressed—or dead," he said in an arrogant voice.

"You sound very angry."

"I am. I can't forgive my father for divorcing my mother, and I don't want to ever see him again," Steve said angrily before hanging up. It was evident that he wanted no contact with his father. He had adopted a tough, independent stance that proclaimed in essence: "I don't need anybody. I can take care of myself." That his father felt abandoned was not his problem. The father was left with one choice—to face the reality of his son's anger that he could not resolve.

❊ ❊ ❊

When parents—primarily mothers—are dealing with abandonment issues, destructive patterns follow: father and mother do not feel appreciated by a child and are unable to find fulfillment with each other. Insecurity about what to do in their relationship makes them dissatisfied partners in marriage. Self-acceptance plays an important part. If parents cannot accept the truth about who they really are and what part they have played in their children's life, they are setting themselves up for disappointment.

At times, excessively high parental expectations are the cause of unhappiness. A widowed mother who had invested years of her life to caring for her son's education and wellness, legitimately expected her son to be able to reciprocate by tending to her needs—a daily phone call, keeping her informed of his new life away from home, and running certain errands. When her son, now moved out of the parental home, found a good job, fell in love, and began to think of his future, he was not as available to his mother. Unaware of her son's daily schedule, one day she decided to tell him how neglected she felt. "Frankie, you never call me as you used to, you never check to see if I'm alive, or if I need anything... you only have one mother, you know." With a chuckle in his voice, Frank replied, "Mother, do you know anyone who has two mothers?" He did love his mother, but he could not be as readily available as he had been. He was going through a personal transition to living on his own.

This is what happens when children leave home, whether they are going to college, getting married, or starting a job that takes them to another part of the country. Parents sense a feeling of abandonment. Abandonment does not mean that a parent is not worth loving or a son or a daughter doesn't care for their parents. Unless there is a major conflict, their physical absence or emotional unavailability is often purely circumstantial and unintentional. The supposedly abandoned parents should not jump at the conclusion that they are not loved. Sensitive parents can take a deeper look into themselves and be content with what were able to contribute in the life of their children. Parental contribution is truly imperative to the growth and stability of children, but when parenting continues in their adult life, young people resent interference and control.

Parents who feel emotionally abandoned by their children may have a deficiency within. That is, they may not feel worthy of being good parents, and are probably starving for acceptance. Their offspring may have a hard time responding efficiently to such a need. If the abandoned parent's need for attention and appreciation is constant, their children will eventually feel burdened and may move away to get away from them. If both parents have similar needs, their expectations rise higher by each encounter with their children and the result can be frustration, disappointment, and anger. It can be of benefit to parents to rediscover their own identity—that is, to seek fulfillment and joy within themselves. Each parent must stand on his or her own feet and accept the reality of their *newness* of life without their children. This is a process that requires patience and discipline. As parent you may find yourself in an empty nest. Do you want to be depressed and wallow in self-pity, or do you prefer to be happy? Start your day by looking at yourself in the mirror. The person you see reflected in the mirror is you. Learn to accept and live with that person the whole day. Forget the person—good or bad parent—you were yesterday, and do not think of who you are going to be tomorrow. Design the quality of life that you can live today. This could give you an awareness of your strengths and how to use them wisely to live a good life for many years. The way to happiness, we can find only within ourselves—not in others.

Many of us expect a great deal from others because we are dependent. We may lack confidence and rely on others—parents, children, friends—to fill the void of our unsatisfied needs. Our demands of others may become overwhelming as we pursue them and then watch as they, our parents, children, and friends, back-peddle in reaction to our needs. As they pull away we project our own desire for wholeness in an emotionally dependent manner, creating a cycle of pursuing and distancing that tends to produce unnecessary anxiety. Eventually, parents have to adjust and seek fulfillment either with their spouses or friends or in the community where they live.

※ ※ ※

I could hardly imagine Monica's situation, being abandoned by her two daughters and spending all her time alone. She lived a life of solitude, but she longed for reconciliation with the two daughters, who were her only family. They've pursued their own dreams and created their own lives independent of her. The pain that she shows when describing her family seeps through her words and paints a portrait of parental abandonment. Her daughters have chosen to disassociate themselves from their mother. While they indulged in their endeavors, Monica longed for their love. She had many needs, but the one she mentioned most was the loss of her family. Maybe just a phone call or a quick visit from either daughter would satiate her social depravity, but as I got to know her, I concluded that this would probably not be enough. She desired their committed communion.

Monica's story reminds me that not only are children being abandoned by their parents (e.g., as orphans), but parents are being abandoned by their children. Growing up, I longed for the same independence as Monica's daughter, but as I became older, I realized the evil aspect of this parental abandonment.

My parents needed me just as much as I needed them. Monica is a beacon set before us to remind us of a much-needed devotion to our families. May our Lord enable us to be less selfish in our lives and be increasingly involved with our families.

Often, we believe that our children or others ought to treat us the way we want them to respond. We may tend to put a relationship on a pedestal, expecting more from an interpersonal relationship than it can deliver. Then when our children or others fail to meet our expectations, we feel betrayed, frustrated, and resentful. When we expect too much from others, we are generally self-critical as well. The part of us that is self-critical is a remnant from childhood that typically represents the echo of one of our parents. The inner critic is the judge and jury of our behavior. It is the part of us that is filled with mandates such as, "you ought to," "you must," "how could you?", "why didn't you?" and so on. Often, instead of taking control of our critic, we project it onto others and make friends feel defective. We may use the same critical terminology on our friends that our parents used on us. It is always a good thing to take responsibility for our critic. We must listen to it, understand its history, and learn to give up its demands. Then we can approach any relationship with realistic expectations.

Invariably, unrealistic expectations are connected to issues of power, manipulation, and control. We might embrace an underlying assumption that says, "People must act the way I want them to, or else I have no use for them." Another twist on this theme is filled with rage and anger: "People better act the way I want them to, or else I will pay them back!" Many times these assumptions underlie patterns of physical and emotional abuse. One parent may try to manipulate and control the behavior of his or her child in order to get what the parent wants. If the abused child refuses, conflict ensues and distance develops between parent and child.

Thoughts You May Consider

- If you are facing some kind of abandonment or rejection by your children or by a significant person in your life at this time, how can you lessen your emotional pain? It would be a mistake to repress it and pretend it is not there. Repression of feelings will negatively influence much of your behavior. Repression is a subtle form of denial to protect you from facing the truth that hurts. At best, see what was your contribution that caused abandonment and, with a sense of humility, seek reconciliation.
- Having realistic expectations of our children involves realizing that all of us are less than perfect. Instead of looking to them to meet our needs, we must take responsibility for our own life and make necessary changes that are in our best interest. We must leave our self-blame behind and find ways to untwist our thinking and behavior to make our lives more fulfilling.
- It is important to value and accept our children for who they are. It is in our best interest not to spend our energy trying to change them to fit an image of what we believe life should be or dictate what we need and what they can provide for us. In their growing years

we gave them roots, as best as we could. It is time to give them wings so they can fly on their own strength.

- Make a sensitive break from the yesterdays—parenting efforts and sacrifices you have made for the wellness of your children—and face the reality of your present life. Capitalize on your personal qualities and realize who you are today: a loving parent. If regrets from your past surface, repair your past as best as you can to feel better.

12

My Own Life as a Father

After high school, I continued my education for another fourteen years in four different schools. I had to take many different courses to be qualified for a doctorate degree in psychology. But as I look back, there was not a single course that taught me how to be a parent. Where did I learn to be a parent? Naturally, from my experience with my parents which over the years I am still trying to improve.

I believe that my life as a responsible adult began on December 9, 1952, the year I became twenty-six years old. On that Sunday morning I entered the ministry as a married man in the Greek Orthodox Church. That was the day parishioners began to call me *Father*, a title assigned to every Greek priest upon his ordination. All of a sudden, I was Father, a leader and role model for many children—most of whom were older and unknown to me. The concept of fatherhood was abstract at first since I was a spiritual father. Understanding my duties was defined by eleven years of seminary life, training in church tradition, Biblical theology, and Christian teachings. This I would have to convey to my congregation in a language that everyone could understand. I did not have to be responsible for anyone's material or physical needs.

Seven months after my ordination, my wife and I were blessed with our first child, a little girl we named Mercene. It was one of the most exciting and yet one of the most sobering events in my life at that time. Besides being a spiritual Father I became a biological father, a co-creator of a new family, connecting past and future in God's creation. At last, I was a total man—even if I did not yet know how to act like a father.

Mercene's birth brought me more responsibilities. I had to learn how to be a caring father and how to model fatherhood in my parish as a priest. In later years I was blessed with three more children, two boys and a second girl. All of them have been more important to me than I have been to them, although they may disagree.

Mercene's presence enhanced my marriage, and developmentally I cherished her growth into adulthood. She was an exceptionally good child, periodically mischievous, and I enjoyed her good humor. Rarely did I need to discipline her, but when she misbehaved I threatened her, *Tha fas xylo,* equivalent to—*you will be spanked.* Giggling, she would respond, *Please, Daddy, don't kill me.* As far as I can recall, I never punished her. Consciously and in my private thoughts I adored her, for she was named after my mother who died when I was less than three years old.

Mercene matured quickly. She was a good student, and attending elementary through high school was a breeze. She graduated from Adelphi University with a master's degree in social work, and she has been working ever since. She is married and has two adult children. Among her hobbies are reading, attending yoga classes, and writing. Many times I share with her topics I intend to write about, and she encourages me to settle myself at my computer and get to work.

Mike is my second child; we named him after my father. From his early years, Mike was a mystery. He always did what he wanted, whenever he wanted. In school he did not obey rules and, therefore, spent a lot of time in the principal's office. At home his behavior and mannerisms reminded me of my own father, who enjoyed spicy meals including hot soup with a dash of salt and pepper. Domestic chores were boring to Mike, and he refused to take any part in them. Schoolwork was not on his agenda; listening to music in his poster-decorated room replaced working on school assignments. Girls loved his company and they kept phoning him, but he preferred to repair and restore cars than to spend time with girls. He was a good artist and won an art contest in our church.

I remember when Mike decided to quit school a year before his graduation. He rebelled against the school system, and he and I argued every day. He threatened to leave home. In the 1970s, life for young people was highly risky: drugs, alcohol, and truancy were rampant. I was scared. I worried so much that I consulted Dr. Herbert Holt, a popular psychiatrist at the time, about the condition of my son. The psychiatrist looked at me with a smile and said, *Your son is growing up. He has to go through many experiences, some of them adverse and unpleasant. You are worrying too much, but you cannot control human nature. It's time to let him grow up. I suggest you give him $500 and say to him, 'Son, go west and come back rich.'*

Noticing my grimace, the psychiatrist said, "You and I left our parents at an early age, and chose to do whatever pleased us. Correct?"

I nodded a silent *Yes,* as he continued. "For a while we became the *prodigal sons,* and our parents worried about us. Away from home we wasted whatever inheritance we received, including sound advice and cultural values. But we woke up one day and decided to return to reality. We faced the truth about parental love, and I think we both did well. Why are you afraid to let your son go?"

It took no further convincing. I let Mike become an adult his own way and make his own decisions. Today, as two mature adults, Mike and I are very close. Often we meet for lunch or dinner. I do admire his accomplishment, such as building a race car and a resort home on a Caribbean island—personal projects he enjoys. Often he asks me when I plan to retire, and I answer, "When the Lord calls me back home." He admires my ambitious attitude: I am eighty-four and still working as a therapist and writing another book. He seems to be proud of me, and I am proud of him. Perhaps I was proud of my father, too, but I never told him so.

Basil, my third child, was a blonde little boy with blue eyes like a Macedonian Greek. People who saw him suggested that I bring him to the attention of movie producers. The idea sounded exciting, but thoughts of exposing my younger son to Hollywood did not appeal to me. I did decide to make a movie about Basil's early life based on a book I authored, *My Beloved Son*. The movie did very well, especially among the Orthodox congregations and related Christian organizations. My ego skyrocketed! I was a proud father seeing my own son on the big screen.

Unlike my other two children, Basil was possessed by a relentless curiosity to learn new things. He could memorize anything and maintained good grades. He loved to read *National Geographic* and could retell, in his own words, scientific facts that interested him. I will never forget that at the age of twelve, Basil stood in front of two hundred young people ages sixteen through twenty-one and delivered a speech about the different parts of the human heart and their functions. His talk was impressive, and once again I felt a proud father.

I do not remember much of Basil's teen years, and repressed the fact that it was a turbulent period for young boys. I moved on to my middle years, going through a troublesome time; re-establishing my own identity as a man, and becoming a responsible father appeared as a priority. Like a trapeze artist in swinging motion, I was letting go of the safe hold of my priesthood in the Church and reaching out to grasp a new profession, psychotherapy. With a leap of faith in a breathless moment between past and future, I let go of security and the familiarity of church life and eventually trusted those who would receive me—scholars of psychology and psychiatry.

At last, the conflicts and the invisible warfare within me faded. I knew that God was already waiting for my return. How did I know? His compassion became real to me as I recalled the words of the prophet Ezekiel, *God does not wish the death of a sinner. Rather, He expects him to return as a repentant* (Ez 33:11). The moment of my return to the Church came. I must acknowledge that once I started my return, I began to wrestle with my procrastination and resistance. Night after night, I fell to my knees and prayed:

> *As the Prodigal Son came back to his father's house and his father welcomed him, embraced and kissed him, likewise I am coming back in tears and beg You, Lord, to receive me. I have sinned against You. I broke my promise to serve You and be a priest till my last breath. I left the altar where I offered services for the salvation of Your people. Lord, have mercy upon me and forgive my unwitting errors. I acknowledge my voluntary and involuntary sins. Genuinely, I admit that I am guilty. But under Your grace I am back, not as a victim of my weaknesses, but as a free son. I am starving for your fatherly acceptance, forgiveness, and love. Amen.*

My thoughts about God's unconditional love brought me back to my senses and gave me the courage to return to Him and be near Him again. At that point, I stayed in frequent touch with Basil, supporting him financially and helping him understand his own state of confusion. Can any teenager truly understand the physical, emotional, intellectual, and spiritual changes he or she has to go through to reach a state of maturity? Where was I, as a loving father or as a mature adult mentor, not there with him to help him find his direction? He most likely felt abandoned during that time.

It was then that I decided to give him what I had never received from my own father or any other adult: I became like the Prodigal Son's father who, *seeing his son in the distance, ran to him, embraced and kissed him and prepared a celebration for him.* Seeing my son's genuine thirst for fatherly love, I hugged and kissed him and told him that I loved him. Under my breath I whispered, hoping he would hear me and believe my words. *I'm the father that has somehow abandoned you. I beg you to forgive me.* I believe he was receptive to my reaching out to him. Feeling accepted and loved, he told me exactly what he wanted me to know.

> *Dad, I know you love me, but you also worry a great deal about me and try to direct my life, telling me what I should or should not do. Thank God I have a good brain; I'm a thinker; I know what I need to do, and I should be allowed to experience life my way. I know I have made mistakes and I will probably make more in my life, but mistakes are lasting lessons.*

Hearing the firmness in his voice, I stopped giving Basil advice or personal wisdom but I never stopped loving him. He became an adult, carried major responsibilities, traveled to foreign lands, and worked hard to support himself.

Katina is my fourth child. She came much later in my life when I had established myself as a psychotherapist, a marriage and family therapist. By that time, although I was far from being perfect, I had become a mature and real father figure in her life. Vividly, I recall the day of her birth, an event that I witnessed with profound awe. When the nurse said, *You can touch your baby now,* with hesitation I extended my hand. As she grabbed on to my index finger, I melted. *Love at first sight.* I bonded with her and kept nurturing this tiny creature with the affections and sacrificial love that was abundantly displayed by her mother. She became *Daddy's little girl.* Noticing my caring for both mother and child, my wife Pat nurtured my fatherhood perception and made me part of a loving parenting team.

It was not long before we were driving Katina to Sun Dance Nursery School. I remember driving her daily and hearing repeatedly on the way her first song, *Jimmy crack corn and I don't care.* Not too long after, it seemed, I saw her walking down the church aisle as a young flower girl in her two cousins' weddings. She became interested in weddings and began to look at pictures in bridal magazines and make plans for her own wedding!

Years went by quickly and Katina blossomed and became my standard for perfection in a woman. She was a most beautiful flower. She thought of me as the perfect father, honoring my birthdays with special gifts and planning surprise parties for my wife and myself on our anniversaries. We took several overseas trips together, and she made sure that we had a good time. She was especially devoted to me and always did things to please me, and to this day she continues to care for my wellness.

I showed my appreciation and reciprocated, making an effort to be discreet with her and respect her privacy and personal desires. I felt real love for her. In my own way I have tried to be a good husband to my wife and a good father to her. I believe that setting beneficial examples enabled Katina to select a good man to be her mate and a father to their children.

Peter, her husband, is an exceptionally wonderful husband, a gentle and generous human being. He genuinely loves our daughter, respects her needs, and is most attentive to their relationship. During the second year of their marriage, they were blessed with the anticipation of having a child.

On October 11, 2008, as I was bringing this chapter to an end, Katina gave birth to a little girl whom they named Stacey. Her arrival brought her parents the greatest possible happiness. Having this gorgeous creature in their midst made them ecstatic. Pat and I, Stacey's grandparents, could not be any happier seeing our daughter's baby the first hour of her life in this world. The new mother's painful labor did not prevent her from a smile of gratitude. Affectionately, she held Stacey and kept looking at her sweet face in wonder—the miracle of birth. *This is my baby! I am her mother!*

Stressed out after she emerged from the birth canal, Stacey fell asleep, wrapped in swaddling clothes and enveloped in an embroidered sheet. Peter took her carefully into his arms and kept admiring the product of his love. *This is daddy's little girl,* he whispered to her before handing her over to us to hold. Instantly Pat and I soared. Stacey's eyes were closed; her chest gently rose and fell as if to murmur *Within me dwells a soul.* Like Simeon in the temple who took Jesus into his arms and praised God, I took Stacey into my arms and gratefully thanked God for his abundant blessings to my family.

Approximately two years later, the happy experience of Stacey's arrival was repeated on August 2010. Katina and Peter were blessed with the birth of a second child, a beautiful little boy whom they named Peter Andreas. The joy this tiny life has brought to our family cannot be described. How grateful can we truly be for God's most precious gift? Grandparents again! Holding this new baby in my arms, I stand in awe, thinking how God's creation continues through us. Another human being, as dependent on God and his mother as our lungs are dependent on oxygen. More or less visible are the riches God has placed within this infant—physical, psychological, moral, intellectual, and spiritual—to be gradually nurtured and developed by God's grace, his parents and the world around it.

As I take an inner inventory of myself as a man, as a husband, and as a father, I realize that I had exaggerated expectations of myself, of my wife, and of my children. I think I did better as a husband, respecting my wife, loving her, and supporting her ideas. Even when we had differences of opinion or disagreements, I strove to be a positive figure in her life and a reasonably caring husband. As a father, I suffered from bouts of anxiety when I noticed any of my children's shortcomings or witnessed some of their risky choices. I wanted my children to make good choices and be happy, in full awareness of my own vulnerability.

Today, one of my lasting joys is to sit with my wife, two daughters and two sons, and their families and chat during casual visits or celebrations. Our conversations include humor and serious talk; we relive memories, they tease me about things they got away with, and they commented on how strict or flexible I was during their growing years. Their presence in my life is rewarding. We interact with each other, less as father and children and more as friends. To me this is God's ultimate blessing. Often I remind them of their growing years, and we laugh a lot remembering the mischief they used to get into and how I used to discipline them.

Recently, I notice that they are interested in learning about my growing years. They want to know in what ways my father influenced me and what methods he used to discipline me when I did something wrong. I find it amusing to tell them stories. Selective as memory tends to be, I pick up episodes from my past that are sometimes humorous and sometimes not. For example, I was late for church one Sunday, and my father slapped me in front of other churchgoers. The hurt of that Sunday's slap was not as painful as it was embarrassing. Another vivid recollection is the corrective belt he used whenever I failed to live up to his expectations; he would pull off his belt to strike me. I was terrified. I can still remember how much it hurt.

One day my father had made plans to take me to work so I could help him harvest olives. He woke me up early and said that we would be leaving in a half hour. Quickly I rolled up a quilt, and placed it on my bed under the covers, to make it look like I was lying there. I hid in the closet and heard him yelling, *Peter! Peter! Aren't you up yet? Now, you're going to get it!*

From a chink in the closet door I watched him as he dashed angrily into my room. He yanked off his belt and struck the rolled quilt again and again. Not hearing my usual cries of pain, he pulled back the covers and saw the trick. Anger turned into laughter, meaning, *You tricked your father. Just wait 'til I catch you.* Beneath the harsh punishments was a sense of humor.

His New Year's message to me when I was nineteen still lives in my memory. I came home in the early morning hours as happy as I could be. I had been out with my friends celebrating the arrival of the New Year, and we had been singing love songs to girlfriends. This was the custom in the

Greek village where I grew up. I saw a cloud of anger in my father's face, as he asked, "Where were you until this early morning hour?"

"Out with my friends."

"With losers. Doing what?"

"Nothing."

"I give up on you. You're hopeless! You'll never amount to anything."

On hearing this story my daughter Mercene exclaimed, "Wow! Dad, you did your share of mischief."

Mike added, "I don't think Dad caused as much trouble as we did. He was pretty normal."

"Thanks, Mike," I said. "When I recall the times I used my belt to punish you when you came home late, I still feel bad about it. Today I want to apologize and ask you to forgive me."

"Dad, I don't remember the belting as much as I remember that never once did you ask where I had been, who I was with, or why I was so late in getting home."

Mike's reply was a lesson. I was eager to punish him without asking where and how and with whom he spent his time. I had inherited that method of discipline from my father. It was cruel, and I should have known better, but where did *my* father learn that method? When he told me how his father disciplined him, I was appalled. One particular time he arrived home in the wee hours of the morning, and when the sun came up, his father tied him with a rope behind a donkey and paraded him through the marketplace. It did not matter that the boy was late because he was chanting at a church vigil, assisting the priest of his parish.

My father's punitive method somehow helped me in a positive way. As an adult, I learned that difficulties and obstacles in life sharpen our skills to face life's challenges. I have worked hard all my life; I have a home and a happy wife; and I have raised a family. Recently, I celebrated my 84rd birthday and am still working as a therapist, exercising regularly, and writing books.

✳ ✳ ✳

In addition to my children's wish to hear what kind of father I had and my desire to tell them, they probably want to know what I think of my relationship with them.

My recent evaluation of myself as a father has been modified over the years. I have admitted to my sons and daughters the fact that I was not a perfect father. As a Christian father, I tried to teach and model for them what I believed to be the values of the Christian faith: love, joy, compassion, generosity, patience, and forgiveness. I want them to be grateful to God for what they have, to accept and love those who are not able to return love, and to find inner joy and peace even in difficult times. I want them to show patience, even when things are not going as well as expected. I want them to practice charity and to be ever mindful of the needs of others.

Of course I no longer have any control over their lives. They are mature, responsible adults, not because of my anxious hovering but, at least in part, because they know I love them. I know my children love me and respect me, but they no longer need my wisdom to design their lives.

There is one more comforting thought to end the chapter. *You are a creature of love. You and I and the whole of humankind are creatures of love—God's love.* In addition to our earthly father with all his imperfections, we have the same one Father, our Loving God, ever present in our lives.

Thoughts You May Consider

- *Give them roots and give them wings* is a popular saying that makes sense. We can give our children a strong and healthy foundation, but it is important to allow them to make decisions of their own and face the consequences of their choices. Young or old, all of us make mistakes, yet we learn more about life from our mistakes than from our successes.
- Psalm 127:3 claims that children are gifts. We do not own them; they have been loaned to us temporarily to raise them up and let them go. Children are like guests in our home. They are not given to us to meet our expectations. They are not here for us; we are here for them until they are grown and on their own, able to meet their own emerging needs.
- Though our children may look and sometimes act like us, they are not us. They do not need to think as we do, nor do they need to always agree with what we say. They are separate human beings and have their own way of thinking, even if their perceptions are wrong according to how we view situations. We are responsible to nurture and guide them, giving them information and few commands.
- As parents, we must see our children through benevolent eyes as God sees us. If you are a parent of more than one child, see each one as unique. Each child has a different personality. Although your children grow under the same roof, and you treat them equally, each has different likes and dislikes, strengths and weaknesses, dreams and goals—threads of uniqueness that weave the one-of-a-kind fabric of each

soul. We must respect our children, pray, and encourage them to become the people God created them to be.

- Children of our times are confused about what they see and hear. Because they are bombarded by technology and exposed to all kinds of electronic devices, we need to understand them and not to be eager to criticize or punish them. They need us to understand them even when their behavior is erroneous. They want our consistent care and unconditional love. Our parental efforts should ultimately serve their best interests, not what is best for us.

13

You Are a Creature of Love

Believe it or not, you are a creature of love, created in the image and likeness of God who is love. Love is your very nature. I have loved you with an everlasting love, claims the Holy Scripture. That love is always the reality of you, abiding in your heart. If you believe that life is for loving, then forgiveness is a rewarding experience in your life, for you will not judge people or take offense at their actions.

God created the human being in his own image and likeness, the Bible claims. In Genesis 1:26–27, we read, *God said, Let us make man in our image, according to our likeness. God created man in His own image; male and female He created them.*

God's wonderful creation of the world is the result of His love. You and I are members of God's creation. We are His children. He created us in and of love. We are creatures of love with an inexhaustible potential for love.

Imagine if all human relationships began with the belief that people are innately wonderful and beautiful—and *with an inner capacity to love.* It may be hard to conceive this, for we may not see this capacity in ourselves. Yet beyond our superficiality we are people with a potential for loving. We need to learn to respect the image and likeness of God in others and be part of love as the one great reality in which we can all live. With practice, we will realize that we can look *through* others instead of just *at* them; and we will understand others as creatures of God with the capacity to love despite some outwardly unloving behaviors. Why take the trouble? Because we do live in the world and because our own peace of mind and health of body and soul are totally dependent on the relationships we establish with others.

It is important to think about how we deal with the people we encounter daily: the janitor or the mail carrier, the garbage collector or the garage attendant, the dentist or the receptionist, or the cashier at the supermarket. Do we see each of us as equals, or do we think of some people as inferior? Long ago, on the mahogany desk of a millionaire's elegant office was a picture of a man in working clothes among portraits of his family. I asked him about the photograph. The millionaire answered, *He's our custodian; I think of him as family.* Confirming the millionaire's attitude, Thoreau said that he could call no man charitable who forgets that the persons who work for him or with him are made of the same clay as himself. To put it simply, we need to move from love platitudes to loving attitudes and actions.

One of our greatest needs is to know that we are accepted and loved. Each one of us has to feel certain, deep down in our heart, that someone loves us, cares for us, and has our best interests at heart. That is a need God designed in us. He wants us to know that He loves every one of us with a passionate intensity too difficult to describe. Our part in life is to learn to love ourselves as God loves us. *Love your neighbor as your self,* our Lord says. This implies that we cannot love anybody if we do not love ourselves.

A father and mother in an intimate moment of love brought about our conception. It was at that moment that God gave us life. Out of love He created us and cares for us. To reassure us of His everlasting love, He sent into the world His only Son, Jesus, whose mission on earth was to teach us how to be and how to love one another. The Bible tells us, *For God so loved the world that He sent His only begotten Son, that those who believe in Him should not perish but have everlasting life* (John 3:16).

In His three years of ministry, Jesus showed us how to live, how to be, and how to love. He called us His *friends* and eventually gave up His life for the sins of the world. With divine authority He said, *My command is this: Love each other as I have loved you. Greater love has no man than the one who lays down his life for his friends. You are my friends if you do what I command* (John 15:12–15).

Jesus left a model we can imitate. I am the way—*I am the path that you should follow, that you may have complete joy within you.* I am the truth—*listen and obey my teaching.* I am the life—*I came to give you real and everlasting life* (John 14:6; italics mine). We cannot be Jesus Christ but we can imitate His virtues of caring, kindness, compassion, forgiveness, and love.

The moment we enter life, we need care and love to survive. It is love that sustains us. Teilhard de Chardin refers to love as the great energy that seeks first to lift each person into wholeness to discover the true self. Second, that love seeks to bring each person into harmony with other persons.

In order to perceive love as energy, we need to understand that love is not something that comes and goes with our changing moods; it is not something that we can fall into or out of, or something that can ever be depleted. Love is an energy emanating from the human soul with purpose: to heal, to harmonize, to invite fellowship with other people, and to create. Erich Fromm, in his book *The Art of Love,* offers excellent thoughts that validate this idea:

Love is not primarily a relationship to a specific person; it is an attitude, an orientation of character that determines the relatedness of a person to the world as a whole, not toward one "object" of love.... If I can say to somebody else, "I love you," I must be able to say, "I love you in everybody, I love through you the world, I love in you also myself."

You may or may not feel that you are capable of being a loving person. Regardless of how you feel, it will be to your emotional benefit to make a conscious effort to start loving. It is a decision that you might have to make when you realize that love is energy already existing within you with fantastic possibilities for a healthier and happier life.

Remember who you are. You are a son or a daughter of a loving Father, God the Creator of the world. Think of the Prodigal Son, *when he came to his senses, his inner self.* He experienced the sudden realization that he was out in a faraway country, cut off from all that was real and cut off from his loving Father. When the awakening occurred, he experienced great joy, anticipating his return. He had been seeking the things that he thought would make his life meaningful. Suddenly he became aware that meaning was not to be found in the world or in things, only in himself. As he took a profound look into himself he realized that he was a son of his father *and a son of God.*

In our yearning to be happy, we may go off into a far country like the Prodigal Son in search of the things that we hope will bring meaning to our lives. This is a great delusion that plagues the lives of most people. It may be the cause of the overemphasis on materialism in our contemporary life. Many people in pursuit of the dream of affluence buy a bigger house, drive a bigger car, belong to a country club, or buy the latest electronic devices; the price they pay is high. Our culture has gloried in the right to pursue happiness. *Pursuit* is not finding or experiencing real joy or peace. Joy can never come through self-indulgence. It only comes through self-realization and gratitude for what is available to us—our potential. It is no wonder that in spite of our abundant wealth, we are often anxious, restless, and unhappy.

Most people seem to be trapped in a work-and-spend cycle. This can be a vicious cycle because people who work more tend to want more and then to buy more. Countless people today are on a "do-more-so-I can-have-more" treadmill. Being busy is a sign of success, and many individuals take pride in being busy. They tend to push themselves to the point of exhaustion, trying to cram more and more activities into an already tight schedule. Author John de Graff calls this *affluenza*—a painful, contagious, socially transmitted condition of overload, debt, anxiety, and waste, resulting from a dogged pursuit of "more."

We need to recognize that everything we own really owns us. The more things we own, the more time and energy we expend on them. In our yearning to own more, we forget that we are guests on this earth and stewards of it while we are here. We forget that God is the Giver of all things. The New Testament declares, *Every good gift and every perfect gift is from above, and comes down from the Father of all lights* (Jas 1:17). God never intended the world to be filled with angry people, murder, violence, disease, and suffering; these are direct results of bad behavior and wrong choices. God created us to be happy people, filled with inner joy and love of life. It is unfortunate when people lose sight of God. To be without God is to lose our greatest source of comfort and coherence.

In spite of human arrogance and disbelief, God took on human form and came to us as Jesus Christ to protect, to teach, and to save us from the destructive powers of disobedience and sin. Jesus said, *It is your Father's good pleasure to give you the Kingdom* (Luke 12:32). Then He adds, *The Kingdom of God is within you* (Luke 17:20).

These are among the most reassuring words given to us. Within you and me exists this dynamic potential for growth. This is the power of God that gives us our "daily bread," from the Greek word, *epiousion,* which means that which is of *essence* in our life.

We need food for our physical sustenance, we need healing for our ailments, and we need guidance for a healthier and happier life. Jesus made clear why He came to earth, lived among His people, and for the believers continues to be invisibly present in our lives. He said, *I have come that you may have life, and that you may have it more abundantly* (John 10:10).

In speaking to His followers, Jesus reassures us, *These things I have spoken to you, that My joy may remain in you and your joy may be complete* (John 15:11).

Studies of positive people show that they rate high on having good relationships with others. Using a positive attitude to help us relate to others may not be an easy concept to incorporate into our lives, but gradually, a more positive attitude will help us discover a deeper potential for love within ourselves. God put it there, and it enables us to think lovingly about persons whom we assume are the cause of our problems. Positive thinking can provide inner peace and a better life for each of us.

This is the day that the Lord has made, I shall rejoice and be glad in it, claims the psalmist (Psalm 128:24). This is *your* day. Be in charge of your thoughts and evaluate your feelings. The morning news, weather reports, traffic conditions, accidents, the ups and downs of the stock market—all indicate that your world is precarious. This often threatens your security and stability. Do not allow mass media to disturb your mind and shape your attitudes. Instead, listen to the voice of God through the mouth of St. Paul who exhorted believers: *Do not be conformed to this world, but be transformed by the renewing of your mind, that you may prove what is good and acceptable to God* (Rom 12:2).

The unnecessary stressors that our culture imposes on us can be overcome as we choose to connect with God in prayer. Many scientists affirm the power of prayer. Jeffrey Graham, Ph.D. refers to the amazing results of prayer and concludes that scientists need to be "open to these phenomena; by validating what we cannot see, hear, or touch, we can refine our extra sensory experience and learn to grow more in these areas."

Of course the Bible clearly teaches the power of prayer: *Be anxious for nothing, but in everything by prayer and supplication, with thanksgiving, let your requests be made known to God; and the peace of God, which surpasses all understanding, will guard your hearts and minds through Christ Jesus* (Phil 4: 4–7).

Take some time at the beginning of the day to be still and connect with your Creator in prayer. Start with a simple verse:

> *Lord our God, we praise you, we bless you, we give thanks to you for this new day. Help us to walk the right path, following your will. Personally, I ask you, Lord, to be at my side today and protect me from negative thoughts. Make this day a time of growth and strengthen me to face the difficult aspects of life with courage and a good attitude. Amen.*

Gradually, this daily practice will enable you to form your own prayers in your own words so that you can speak to God as you would speak to a very intimate and loving friend. Then, walk into the world with a smile on your face. Of course, when your associates or friends see the smile they may say, *What makes you so happy?* If you answer, *I'm a child of God. He makes my life possible and has my best interests at heart for me. He loves me,* others may think that you came from another planet. You may have to restrain the manner in which you outwardly express your exuberance and the overflow of your love. Probably, people who challenge your smile are unhappy within themselves. They are not aware that they, too, are children of a loving God.

Many people in their quest for love, meaning, and happiness take trips around the world to see things they think will be rewarding. Who can question the fact that there are beautiful places in the world? People who can freely travel to exotic places can be grateful that they are able to have such experiences. In reality, though, most people do not have the means for such travel, and yet they are able to find fulfillment in simple vacations. What is of importance is to find something rewarding in every new experience.

Recently, a couple I know well returned from a safari in Africa. I asked them how they enjoyed such an adventurous vacation. *Oh, those poor people! How can they live like that? They have nothing to be happy about. The conditions are absolutely terrible* were their comments. This couple saw only the dark side of Africa.

In a church mission, I also had a chance to travel to different parts of Africa with my family. Truly, I witnessed poverty and lack of many things—food, clothing, and medicine—that other nations have in abundance. But I also experienced a simple yet genuine hospitality, a joyous spirit among many people who were barefoot and poorly dressed. They did not need to have many possessions to be happy. They were conscious of their love of life. I saw their participation in church services—singing and clapping their hands as their voices demonstrated that they were completely connected with God. The melody of their hymns seemed to come from a choir of angels praising God.

I often wonder what it takes to make a human being happy and loving. We live in a world of change. Trying to resist life's course is like swimming against a powerful current. Why try to change life's happenings? Your age is what it is, your physical stature is what it is, you are who you are, and it is good. Accept it. Rejoice in it. The key to continuity of joy in life is to turn within and become aware of God 's power within us. Can you accept this truth, that *it is your Father's good pleasure to give you the kingdom* (Luke 12:32)?

Can you accept the truth that you are a child of God, who loves you with an everlasting love? Can you believe the truth that God has created you in His image and likeness, endowing you with infinite possibilities, and not be joyful? Listen to His voice through St. Paul's Letter to the Romans:

> *Who will separate us from the love of Christ? Will hardship, or distress, or persecution, or famine, or nakedness, or peril, or sword? For I am convinced that neither death, nor life, nor angels, nor rulers, nor things present, nor things to come, nor powers, nor height, nor depth, nor anything else in all creation, will be able to separate us from the love of God in Christ Jesus our Lord* (Rom 8:35–39)

Thoughts You May Consider

- God designed you as a creature of love, and His plan continues to be to restore the joy and love He created within you. Do you want to live a healthier life and live longer? Feel the inner joy that Jesus spoke about and say to yourself, *I am a child of God. He created me out of love, and I can be happy knowing that God loves me. My part is to develop a loving attitude.*
- If you were to think for a moment and believe that God has His eyes fixed constantly on you, your thoughts would be more serene, your heart would be at peace, your conduct would be irreproachable, and your service for the benefit of others could be altruistic.
- You can be more loving when you learn to think on the positive side of life more often. Let go of yesterday's misfortunes and tragedies and recollect some of the good things that happened in your life. Loving people have more social contact and better social relationships than their unloving counterparts.
- To many of us whose image suffers from past mistakes or sins and guilt, Jesus responds by offering forgiveness and release from the burdens we carry. *Come to Me, all who are weary and heavy laden, and I will give you rest. Take my yoke upon you, and learn from Me, for I am gentle and humble in heart; and you shall find rest for your souls. For my yoke is easy, and My load is light* (Matt 11:28–30).
- Embraced by God's love, every morning as you awaken to a new day you can view the world as a place for challenge and opportunity. Henry Drummond says, *Is*

not life full of opportunities for learning love? The world is not a playground; it is a schoolroom. Life is not a holiday, but an education. And the one eternal lesson for us all is how better we can love.

14

You Can Be Reconciled

People who seek reconciliation discover that it removes difficulties, looks for the positive in the other, and gives courage for the despondent and strength for the weak. Reconciliation is like that certain star that is guiding the seafarer through the darkest night. Regardless of how hurt we are, we need to move on and pursue healing. If we accept the challenge to let go of painful events, we may cherish the gifts of peace and reconciliation.

Feelings of abandonment or loneliness can only find relief when we come to be in good standing with God our Creator. When we leave God out of our daily life or turn to Him only in dire need, God does not abandon us. Why? Because He loves us and wants us to know who He really is in our life. Every hour of each day, He continues to care as a father cares for his children. God loves the just and shows mercy upon the sinners; He wants to be part of our lives, help us refine our thoughts and cleanse our minds, and deliver us from all adversities, evil, and stressful situations.

A story is told about Father George, known as Papayiorgi. He was a humble priest who years ago was assigned to be a chaplain in a colony of lepers on a Greek island. His limited theological training was compensated for by his strong faith in God and his commitment to serve the afflicted. One Good Friday, in his eagerness to explain the Passion story, Father

George nailed on the cross a colorful and graphic effigy of the body of Christ in the form of leper. When his bishop heard about this, he reprimanded him. *How dare you defile the body of our Lord making Him appear as a leper? That's blasphemy.* Gently, the priest replied, *Your eminence, how else could I make these lepers understand that God really loves them, except by making Christ like one of them?*

The bishop shook his head. The message was clear. To reassure us of His love, God becomes one of us in Jesus Christ, regardless of our emotional and physical condition, Do we want to feel God's presence in our life? If we answer yes, then we have to think about Him, study His teachings, glean as much as we can of His wisdom, and visualize Him close to our hearts.

After the disobedience of our progenitors, Adam and Eve, when humanity reached the peak of corruption, God became man and entered our world as Jesus Christ to bring peace and salvation. In John 3:16 we read, *For God so loved the world that He sent his only Son, so that everyone who believes in Him may not perish but may have eternal life.* Christ's amazing teachings continue to be our source of strength, comfort, joy, and peace. One scriptural part that defines most accurately God's love for each one of us is the familiar story of the Prodigal Son. It has been said that if all four Gospels were lost and the only surviving fragment contained the story of the Prodigal Son, that would be sufficient evidence that the author was our God.

Each time we read about the Prodigal Son a number of challenging emotions are evoked in our hearts. Several aspects of this story resemble our life. First, we think of the father's predicament. Here is the younger son demanding a portion of the inheritance that his father planned to give him. Knowing his son's vigor and vitality, did he want him to leave his home and those caring for him? Of course not! Yet the father willingly gave him part of his inheritance. Perhaps as a caring father, he held back his own emotions about his son's departure. Young, inexperienced, and naïve, most likely spoiled, the son to whom he had given freedom and special favors, now was going far afield without a thought for his father's breaking heart.

In order to escape parental control and family expectations, the Prodigal Son went to a foreign land, far from fatherly guidance and protection. Many of us abandon God's presence and go far away where we know no one knows us, where everything is permitted. Not being accountable to anyone, we expose ourselves to mass media's seductions, distortions, theaters, silly and superficial parties, and TV programs of violence and corruption. We are influenced by clever ads propagated by today's greedy merchants who praise their products, exploiting beautiful women and sex. God's name is never mentioned. It is a life of superficiality and loose living, permeated by a doctrine of instant satisfaction.

The Prodigal Son devoured his inheritance in the company of derelicts and prostitutes and became destitute. Currently, we feel just as confused as this young man since every day we substitute kindness with indifference, negativity, and even hostility. Having taken advantage of the gifts God has given us—our daily life, our freedom, our talents—we drag ourselves into despair. We become selfish, critical, and irritated by other people's behavior. The words of St. Paul echo in our ears: *Wretched man that I am, who will save me from this misery?*

The Prodigal Son took the path that led him into darkness, where he became lost. Somehow, we become present-day prodigal sons. We waste God's gifts of joy, peace, and love; we ignore His abundant blessings; we walk in darkness and waste our lives.

In spite of our behavior, God graciously gives us life, choices, opportunities, talents, and virtues, and above all, the gift of the Holy Spirit to direct our lives. As a benevolent Father, God gives such gifts to all His children because He is not only God of love, He is also God of freedom. He wants us humans to have free will and to be responsible for our choices.

The Parable of the Prodigal Son can help us understand the stages in our journey to reconciliation with God, if we ever want to enjoy peace and contentment. The journey for the young man in the parable begins with selfishness. His arrogance takes him from the home of his parents—as our arrogance takes us from the shelter of God's grace and the Christian life into the desert of indifference. His major concern in his new self-centered lifestyle is himself and his personal gratification. None of the relationships he establishes are lasting. When his money runs out, so do his friends. Eventually he discovers himself alone, mired in the mud of a pigpen, starving, and eating food fit only for pigs. Then comes this significant phrase in the story: *Coming to his senses at last...*

This can be the beginning of our journey back, the beginning of our reconciliation with God. It is a process of inner change. This change begins with a *coming to one's senses,* with a realization that all is not right with our values and style of life. Prompted by our faith, we respond to God's call. This initiates a desire for change. *Metanoia,* the term the New Testament uses, suggests an internal turnabout, a change of heart that is revealed in one's conduct. The Greek verb *metanoetai* means *commands our attention to change our mind.* Changing the way of our thinking implies interior transformation that comes about when God's Spirit touches our lives with the Good News that God loves us unconditionally. Our part in this saving action is to be open to the gift of God's love—to be receptive of His grace.

Feeling this inner change is always a response to being loved by God. In fact, the most important part of our transformation is the joyful experience of being loved and realizing that God's love is available to us. Our journey back to God is not a once-in-a-lifetime moment but a continuous, ongoing, lifelong process that brings us ever closer to holiness and love. Each experience of moral change prompts us to turn more and more toward God, because each change-of-heart experience reveals God in a new, brighter light.

As we examine our values, attitudes, and style of life, we discover that we are missing the mark. Having gone astray, we experience the next step in our journey: guilt followed by contrition. This step of changing direction helps us break away from our bad attitudes and damaging habits, lying, cheating, hypocrisy, or anger. We leave these behind and make resolutions for a better future. Changing direction means examining our present relationships in the light of God's love, and taking the necessary steps to repair those damaging relationships with others and restore our relationship with God. When we are faced with temptations, we can ask the Holy Spirit that abides in each one of us to help. No matter how big or small the problem, we can overcome it with God's help. Persons who genuinely turn to God will never be the same again, because being reconciled with God implies transforming the way we relate to others, ourselves, the world, the universe, and God. Unless we can see that our values, attitudes and actions are in conflict with the Christian ones, we will never see a need to change or desire to be reconciled.

As we think of the way the father unconditionally accepted his son's departure and the joyful manner in which he ordered a big celebration for his return, we may perceive God differently, as a compassionate Father who might be waiting for our awakening. Our thoughts about His unconditional love may bring us back to our senses and give us the courage to come back and be near Him. It is possible that once we start our return, we may begin to wrestle with procrastination and resistance. Within us abides a strange feeling of pride leading us in a demonic direction away from God, weakening us, and causing despair. But we do have a choice to prepare ourselves for self-examination and genuine repentance. As a result, the conflicts and the unseen warfare within us will fade out. God is already waiting for our return. How do we know? Because His compassion becomes real to us as we recall the words of the prophet Ezekiel: *God does not wish the death of a sinner. Rather, He expects him to return as a repentant.*

Let's look again at our story. The young man takes the first step—*he comes to his senses,* overcomes his blindness, and sees what he must do. Before he ever gets out of the pigpen, he admits his sinfulness, saying to himself, *I'm going back to my father, and I will say to him, "Father, I have sinned against God and against you…. Treat me like one of your hired hands."* Some people may find it difficult to believe the meaning of the story because of the human condition. The father welcomes the son back instantly. He doesn't even wait for him to get to the house. "Quick!" says the father. "Let us celebrate. My son is back ready to admit his sins, but I don't want to hear them. He returned to me; let's celebrate." Celebration makes sense only when there is really something to celebrate. In this parable it is imperative to notice the concept of reconciliation. Look how Jesus portrays our heavenly Father in this parable. The father, seeing his son in the distance, runs out to meet him with an embrace and a kiss. Through one loving gesture, the father forgives the son even before the son makes his confession! When he does, it seems the father hardly listens. The confession is not the most important thing here; the important thing is that his son has returned. The son need not beg for forgiveness; he has been forgiven. This is the glorious

Good News: God's forgiveness, like God's love, doesn't stop. Jesus reveals to us a loving God who can simply forgive! God really is like the merciful parent in this parable. God is not out to catch us in our sin and punish us; He is reaching out in spite of our sin to bring us back to Him, where there is abundant love.

Reconciliation is not just a matter of getting rid of sin or of feeling forgiven. It is rather the realization that God's infinite mercy permeates and heals our ailing souls. Reconciliation is often a long, painful process. Admitting our sins is one aspect of the process. It is actually the external expression of the interior transformation that the change of mind has brought about in us. *Confess your sins to each other and pray for each other so that you may be healed* (James 5:16). To confess implies disclosing and acknowledging something damaging or discomforting to yourself. It also means revealing your wrongdoing to God, to a priest, to a minister of the church, or to a spiritual counselor. As you admit and divulge your guilt, you regain relief and peace of mind. It is a journey inundated with challenges and choices, but its destination is to be a participant in God's Kingdom.

A question that often arises is: *Why confess my sins?* And why confess to a priest or to anyone? Why not confess directly to God, since God has already forgiven me anyway? From God's point of view, the simple answer is: *There is no reason.* But from our point of view, the answer is that as human beings who do not live in our minds alone, we need to externalize bodily—with words, signs, and gestures—what is in our minds and heart. We need to see, hear, and feel forgiveness—not just think about it. We need other human beings to help us externalize what is within and open our hearts before the Lord. This puts confessors in a new light. They are best seen, not as faceless and impersonal judges, but as guides in our discernment, compassionately helping us experience and proclaim the mercy of God in our life. God's offer of unconditional forgiveness to anyone, any sinner who comes to Him, makes us feel good psychologically. Whether we know it or not, want it or not, in the face of such love and forgiveness we may feel uncomfortable. It creates a pressure within us that makes us feel we should *do something* to deserve such largess—or at least feel a little bit guilty or be punished. God's love is a free gift and is available to all those who are willing to receive it.

Nikos Kazantzakis novelizes the story of *The Last Judgment:* Christ has come again with glory to judge the living and the dead. He is sitting on a glorious velvety throne, surrounded by a cloud of angels, and he separates the righteous people from the sinners, as a shepherd would separate the sheep from the goats. The righteous he puts on his right and the sinners on his left. Then he commands the angels to escort the righteous into the Kingdom that he has prepared for them. Next, he turns to those on his left hand and says, *Depart from me, you cursed, into the eternal fire prepared for the devil and his angels.* As they are about to be thrown into eternal fire, Mary looks at Jesus with compassionate eyes. *Son!* she says. Christ instantly knows what his mother has in mind. The judgment stops. Anxiously, the sinners look at the Great Judge. Christ looks back at his mother, nods, and smiles. Mary's gentle voice resounds across the sky: *My Son is not just a God of Justice, he is also a God of mercy and love.* Christ shakes his head and orders his angels to let the sinners enter his Kingdom.

A novelist may use poetic license to make a story interesting. Kazantzakis simply offers his perception of God's love. Believers, on the other hand, use their background and faith to see what is true and noble. If we have not been loved in our growing years, and if we have not learned how to love, it is so hard for us to perceive God's love. All we need is to hear Christ's words during his last hour on the cross. *Today, you are with Me in Paradise,* He said to the thief who had acknowledged his sinful life. *Your sins are forgiven,* He said to the paralytic. The Scribes and the Pharisees who were present objected. *Who can forgive sins but God?* At another time, Christ forgave the woman who was about to be stoned because she had committed adultery. *Let the one who has no sin cast the first stone,* He said to her accusers, who one by one walked away. *Go and sin no more,* He said. His presence among people was a ministry of love and forgiveness, a mission to reconcile us with one another and with God.

If we knew how to listen to Christ, we would hear Him speaking to us. He speaks in his Gospels. He also speaks to us through life—that new gospel to which we ourselves add a page each day by behavior and lifestyle. A practical way that will help us listen and feel reconciled with him is to imagine what He would say if He Himself interpreted His Gospels for you and me today. *I come into your world today to bring you My peace and joy, to strengthen you in difficult times. Have you been wronged, hurt, betrayed, blamed, accused, emotionally blackmailed, lied to? Allow me to show you a different way of life, because I love you unconditionally.*

Think of a time when you were *in love* with your partner or a significant other. This seemed to be the happiest state. Life became meaningful, and you felt fulfilled because someone met your needs and made an effort to please you. Someone made you feel special, and you reciprocated to him or her. What the world out there thought of your relationship did not matter, because each time you were together, you felt whole. As long as you met each other's emerging needs, your state of love was intense. Suddenly, something went wrong. An argument, a disagreement or conflict of interests surfaced, and the intense love turned into pain and intense grief. Human love is conditional and can easily become anger and hostility. Only God's love is everlasting and under any condition available to you and me. What we all need is faith in God, who offers us the capacity to love ourselves and even love others who have been unloving to us.

If our faith tends to be anemic, it disrupts our relationship with God and our relationship with others as well as with ourselves. There is something we can do to restore and revitalize our faith. Remember our roots, our heritage. We are created in the image of God. He wants his creation to be complete. When we relate to his Son, Jesus Christ, in faith, we have potential for a sense of inner wholeness. This is the new life that Christ promises through the voice of the Apostle Paul: *Clothe yourselves with love, which binds everything together in perfect harmony. Let the peace of Christ rule your hearts* (Col 3:14–15).

This is the ultimate gift in our lives, that God is the God of love. He loves us with a kind love that is not turned off by bad behavior, our failures, our faults, or our weaknesses. We are not just insignificant beings or animals to be used or insects to be crushed. We are not miserable offenders cowering in remote corners to avoid punishment. We are human beings loved by God Himself. His love reaches us, not because we have earned it through our charitable efforts, not because we have done something worthwhile in our lives, but because of what God is and because of what Christ has done for us—offering unconditional acceptance, compassion, love, and forgiveness. Having been forgiven, we are empowered to forgive ourselves and to forgive one another, heal one another, and celebrate the fact that together as his family, we have come a step closer to God.

When we experience reconciliation, we become the heralds of Christ's Kingdom on earth.

Thoughts You May Consider

- Human beings are the objects of God's love. He sustains the universe, gives us life, and chooses humans to be his children. He endows us with the potential to be happy. He invests goodness and power to make each one of us a co-creator and a true friend. *Greater love has no man than the one who lays down his life for his friends.* This is what Christ said and did.
- Our part is to love one another as God loves us and learn how to love and forgive. *How can I forgive a person who has caused me so much pain? It is difficult, because my memory brings back the event that caused me pain.* Facing the emotional pain in our hearts can be frightening. Yet the possibility of forgiveness offers relief and hope of moral freedom when we are in the grip of bitterness and despair.
- If something hurtful has happened that distanced you from a friend or your spouse, and you want to restore the relationship, what can you do? If you are the offender, you go to the one you have offended and express genuine regret. You want to heal the wounds or resolve the conflict. If the other person is the offender and you wish to reconnect with that person, you muster up enough courage to forgive the offending person.

- There is something we can do about the unconditional forgiveness we receive from God: forgive others as we have been forgiven. Having been forgiven, we are empowered to forgive ourselves and to forgive one another, heal one another, and celebrate the fact that together we have come a step closer to God.

- Reconciliation does not bring about something that was absent. It proclaims and enables us to own God's love and forgiveness, which are already present. When you are able to say *Lord, I accept your forgiveness. Enable me to forgive myself,* the following prayer will pave the way for your reconciliation with God.

A Prayer That Can Bring Joy
And Peace To Your Heart:

*As the Prodigal Son came back to his father's house,
and his father welcomed him, embraced and kissed him,
likewise I am coming back in genuine repentance and plead
with You. Lord, I have sinned against You. Have mercy
upon me and forgive all my sins and unwitting errors.
I acknowledge my voluntary and involuntary sins.
Genuinely, I admit that I am guilty. But I'm back
under Your grace, not as a slave of my passions,
but as a free person. I am starving for Your fatherly
acceptance and love. Please feed my soul with
Your precious presence. Fill my life with the fruits
of the Holy Spirit—love, joy, peace, patience,
kindness, generosity, faithfulness, gentleness,
and self-control. I know that in Your unfathomable love,
You will accept me and embrace me as one of Your
children who, at last, came to his senses and now
needs the kiss of forgiveness. Amen.*

15

Intimacy with Jesus Christ

Nothing in human history is able to equalize the love which Jesus inspired, the solace which He spread, the compassion which He engendered, the hope which He kindled in the breast of humanity.

—Rabbi H. G. Emelow

Intimacy with Jesus implies that we become aware of His presence in our life. Through prayer, involvement in charity work, and imitating His life, we connect with Him. We will sense inner joy being in frequent contact with our Creator. As we believe and trust our life in Jesus, our heart will hear His voice: I am with you always. You are never alone. I am more present in your life than the sunrise is to the morning. I am more present in your life than water is to the ocean. I am more present in your life than the sun is to the light. I am in you and with you and nothing can separate us.

Our human nature ever craves for an intimate friend. We look for someone whom we can be with and share life as it unfolds before us daily. When we find such a person with whom we can spend time, discussing common goals, and sharing secrets, successes, or failures, and happy or unhappy events, eventually we have attained an intimate relationship. The absence of such a friend leaves us hollow, shallow, or enslaved to a hectic schedule that never lets up. The desperate need in our times is not for a larger number of important acquaintances, but at least for one true friend.

The story of Diogenes points out this need. During daylight he held a lit lantern and walked in the streets of Athens saying, *I'm looking for an honest man*. Most likely he was looking for a good friend. More convincing about this need of having someone in our life who truly cares is the story of the paralytic (John 5:1–15). In Jerusalem by the pool of Bethesda, there was a man who had been ill for thirty-eight years. He was waiting for someone to put him into the pool at the time when the angel stirred the water so that he could get well. When Jesus asked him, *Do you want to be well?*, the paralytic answered, *Sir, I have no man [caring enough] to put me into the pool at the right time*. Jesus said to him, *Rise, take up your pallet, and walk*. The paralytic was instantly healed, and he took up his pallet and walked.

If you have grown weary of superficial things and temporary satisfactions, and you feel tired of surface talk and shallow thinking, you may be on the verge of emotional paralysis. Deep down in your heart, you know there has to be something more; you are just not sure how to get it. One thing is certain: You do not want to stay where you are now. Just as Jesus stood in front of the paralytic and asked him, *Do you want to become well?*, He is standing before you and me this very moment, asking us if we want healing from our nagging ills. Harassed by the demands of life, exhausted, we look around us for relief, a place where we could be quiet, where we could be refreshed and revitalized. Our hearts yearn for new strength to go on living a more pleasant life. All we need is to see Jesus with the eyes of faith and accept the invitation to come close to him.

Intimate relationship is a much desirable state. It is a true interaction with a friend, a soul mate, whose company we cherish. Intimacy encourages and strengthens human relationships. When we wonder whom we could have an intimate relationship with, we feel sensitive about personal exposure. If we appear over-enthusiastic, we may innocently share our inner core, revealing undesirable parts of our self, blunders, guilty feelings, or foolish things we have done. As a result, our self-esteem and the esteem others have for us diminish. Fear of being misunderstood or rejected by an intimate other causes us to alienate or isolate ourselves. Does this mean that we cannot have an intimate relationship? Of course not. We can, as long as we do not take intimacy lightly. Everyone needs a relationship with another person who accepts us lovingly and unconditionally. Think of how many times we simply assume that someone in a business partnership or relationship is honest and will not let us down. We believe them because we have faith when they say they are honest. Later, they may turn out to be untrustworthy or they may betray us. It would be a state of bliss if we could come across a human being who could honestly say to us, *I love you just the way you are.* Is there such a person?

Intimacy with Jesus brings greater fulfillment to our life. It is a promise. It is His desire to see us happy. The question is: Do we want to be happy? Like the paralytic, do we want to have a life of wellness? We know the answer. Yes, you and I want to be well and happy. But how can we be happy if we do not listen to the voice of Jesus who uses our conscience to keep us on the right road? How can I be happy if I do not sense the peace of Christ within me, or if I have serious reasons to believe that I need to change something in my life? Can I be happy if I do not respect my neighbor, if I tend to be critical and judgmental and fail to recognize my own weaknesses? Can I be happy when I am angry and bitter? If I constantly make demands on others, whether in the name of propriety or justice, will I feel happy? Can I be happy if I lack temperance and I complain about everything and for nothing?

What about my immediate others? *Can I be happy if I cannot make amends and reconcile with members of my own family?*, as one of my clients asked.

It is even harder to relate honestly to someone with whom we have a close relationship. A husband I am currently counseling said the following. *When I have a conflict with my wife, and I feel angry, disappointed, or misunderstood, I do not feel safe letting my true feelings show. I walk away angry and hurt. It is hard not to brood over it. I question whether my efforts to discuss the conflict add to estrangement, so I prefer to distance myself from the situation.* Truly, feeling isolated or rejected hurts. We may withdraw from conflictual situations, we may isolate ourselves from people, but we can never hide from God. He is everywhere present. Listen to what the psalmist has to say: *Where can I go from Your Spirit? Or where can I flee from Your presence? If I ascend to heaven, You are there; if I descend to the depths of the sea, You are there* (Psalm 139:7–8).

We believe in the existence of God who, in time, took on human flesh, became man, and revealed himself to his people as Jesus Christ. We recognize Jesus as creator, provider of all good things. We believe in the purpose and value of His death on the cross, the glory of His resurrection, and we believe in His capacity to save us from our sins and to sanctify us. As a Redeemer, Christ is always determined to preserve, improve, and protect us. As a Savior, He is always in the process of adjusting, repairing, stimulating, and encouraging. As a Sanctifier, He clarifies objectives, stirs up our inclinations, awakens ideals, giving us the energy to act, to be useful, giving us ideas and the capacity to create that we may experience the joy of building something new. All these aspects of God's presence in our lives require only an ordinary faith, an everyday faith. Those of us who have been baptized and raised by Christian parents, or have grown up in a Christian community, belong to God. We have been immersed into his love; we have an intimacy that replaces any feeling of abandonment or loneliness.

Most of us believe that God is merciful. It would be hard to exaggerate how important this realization is to all of us in our human frailties. Anger, fear, and hate hinder our relationship with God. We can hardly relate with a person when these negative feelings get in the way. Will God reject me if sometimes I am afraid of Him? Will God punish me if sometimes I am angry at Him because He does not answer my prayers? How can I say I want God's love when I have these feelings? Does my inner anguish for the dark stuff that lurks inside me mean that God has abandoned me? God does not abandon anyone. Has Christ ever ignored or rejected anyone who sought his help? It is through Christ that energy and the power of divine love find their way into our lives and transform us, making us better people, stronger, and wiser, and keeping us in His grace. All this is possible as we connect with Jesus in faith and prayer.

It is a comfort to recall the words of Jesus: *If your brother has anything against you, leave your gift at the altar and go first and be reconciled with your brother.* Does that mean that Jesus will reject me? Of course not. Jesus accepts, enlightens, loves, and sanctifies every human being who wishes to know the truth. He says: Whoever wishes to come after Me must deny himself, take up his cross and follow Me (Mark 8:34; cf. Luke 9:22). If I want to be loved by God, I have to let go of the angry and arrogant self. Jesus also says, *Whoever follows Me will not walk in darkness, but will have the light of life* (John 8:12). If I don't want to walk in darkness, I had better listen to what Jesus said when Peter asked, *Lord, how often should I forgive? As many times as seven?* Jesus answered him: *Not seven times, but, I tell you, seventy-seven times.*

At some time, someone may have disappointed us. We do not want that to happen again, so we become cautious as we interact with others. With Jesus we do not have to be cautious. He can pull us out of the difficult situations a dozen times. It may sound too good to be true. If we can trust Him with our salvation—our eternal destiny—we can surely trust Him with our everyday life. Building intimacy with a person takes time, effort, and emotional availability. What will it take to develop intimacy with Jesus Christ? You and I have to want it enough to include Him in our daily life. It is essential to reorder our private life, and that requires us to slow our pace as well as stop being influenced by contemporary attractions. Literally, we need to relax, rest, let go of seeking more money or material wealth. These initial steps are difficult and require discipline. Every day we are challenged in this world of restlessness, noise, traffic, and continuous activity, which make discipline unattainable. In spite of the complexities of life, you and I can enter into an intimate relationship with Jesus, whose voice resounds, *Come unto me all of you who work hard and are heavy laden, and I will give you rest.* This invitation is extended to people of every race, color, culture, and faith: people of any level of maturity and age, people who are employed or unemployed, single or married people with children or without children; all people who realize that we are children of God. Our part is to be alone, surrender to His care, and keep silent so we can hear His voice.

Start today, and tell Jesus you want to have a close, intimate relationship with him. If I were to describe my own relationship with Jesus, I would say that first, of course, He is my Savior and Redeemer, but I would also call Him my Best

Friend, my Brother, my Mentor, and my Companion in the journey of life. I firmly believe He does not want an arm's length relationship with any of his followers, men or women. He wants us to love Him with our whole heart as He loves us. He wants us to trust him.

Since Jesus knows us better than we know ourselves, He also knows that it will take time to develop trust in who He is in our lives. One of the best ways we can listen to God is through his Word, the Bible. If you have the right kind of Bible, you'll find it easy to understand and apply to your day-to-day life. The more you read the Bible, the better you know the mind of God. Jesus reveals His ways and His Father's ways through this holy book. As we noted earlier, many people who read the Bible for the first time discover that God is much kinder, gentler, and compassionate than they thought.

An intimate relationship is a one-on-one relationship, with no distractions. To build intimacy with Jesus, we must spend time alone with Him. We have to want it enough to stop all the noise. God's presence is felt the moment we take the Bible in our hands and start reading it. The Holy Spirit will direct our reading and give us the insights he wants us to have. Read and meditate on what the psalmist has to say. Note the yearning of his heart as he invites God to probe into his innermost thoughts:

> *O Lord, you have searched me and known me.*
> *You know when I sit down and when I rise up;*
> *You discern my thoughts from far away.*
> *You search out my path and my lying down,*
> *and are acquainted with all my ways.*
> *Even before a word is on my tongue,*
> *O Lord, you know it completely.*

Search me, O God, and know my heart;
test me and know my thoughts.
See if there is any wicked way in me,
and lead me in the way everlasting.

Psalm 139:1–4, 23–24.

Jesus does not demand perfection in order to respond to our needs. He accepts us as we are, at the very moment we turn to Him. He did not come into the world for the healthy; He came for those who needed emotional, mental, and physical healing. He came to seek out the lost sheep. His heart overflows with compassion for us. We do not have to wait until we become perfect to call upon Jesus. We can come close to him with our fears and disappointments, with our broken or sick hearts, and with our faith that is shaky and apparently lacking ardor. He waits for the little interest we have, be it weak or enthusiastic. Jesus is aware of our human limitations, but His love repairs our broken hearts and rekindles ardor and vigor in our faith. In a prayer, he says: *Father . . . I wish that where I am they also may be with me . . .* (John 17:24).

When you understand, when you believe that I am in you, that I live the will of my Father in you, you will no longer speak of solitude and isolation. I am in you; be aware of this. Your life will become mine, and you will that all that is mine is yours. (cf. John 17:10). Our relationship with Him depends upon us, because He is always present and attentive. He is always present in each one of us because we are created after His image and likeness.

We sense God's presence as we pray. Our prayer is an affirmation of His presence. When we take time to pray, sooner or later prayer becomes part of our life. In the beginning our prayers may be brief, lacking content or focus, but after a while, we find ourselves staying longer in prayer. In the company of a good friend, we are not aware of how rapidly time goes by. Likewise, being in God's presence, time is no longer an issue, for the feeling is exuberant. Jesus appears to us in perceptible fashion. He is ever present where we are. He goes where we go. He comes to where we walk, where we work, where we eat, where we sleep, where we love, where we have fun, where we exult, or where we suffer. He is actively present in us with His affection, His efficacy, His compassion, His love, His mercy, and His tenderness.

As God, Jesus is everywhere. His humanity is the instrument by which He reaches others, there where they are—in the depths of their condition, their life, their joy, their sorrow, and their exultation. His beneficial presence is everywhere. Jesus, by his divine-human nature—attentive, delicate, and fascinating—adapts to all situations; among His apostles we find sinners whom He accepts and forgives. In His earthly life, He gives attention to everyone—the rich, Zacchaeus, the centurion, the scholars, Nicodemus, Joseph of Arimathea, Simon the leper, sinners, Mary Magdalene, the woman caught in adultery, the Samaritan, and the thieves on the cross. All those who seek Him are healed; He loves to sow joy, peace, and assurance of salvation in their hearts. He heals the paralyzed, the lame, the lepers, and the blind; He raises the only son of the widow, the daughter of Jairus, and Lazarus.

You and I are a continuation of His humanity. It is within our endowment to let Jesus live through us, imitating His life and continuing His work of salvation.

I have no way of knowing how this book came into your hands. And I will never know what it meant to you as you read it. But I am sure of this: You, like me and other readers, wrestle with life's challenges and need to be reminded that we are not alone. Jesus is ever-present in our life, inviting us to take the path of the inner truth. That means taking responsibility for everything that is in our life: for what pleases us and for what we are ashamed of, for the rich person inside us and for the poor one. Most of us strive for external acceptance, when the only acceptance that is important is internal. There is no need to prove ourselves to others. We need to love ourselves completely and unconditionally as God loves us. Then nothing can shake us. St. Francis of Assisi calls this *loving the leper within us.* If we learn to love the poor one within us, we will discover that we have room to have compassion outside, too—that there is room in us for others, for those who are different from us, for the least among us brothers and sisters. Compassion is the basis of all truthful relationships. It means being present with love for ourselves and for others. Think for a second: who in your life needs you today?

Thoughts You May Consider

- Whatever our state of mind or body, a brief prayer can always connect us with the Giver of life. A few simple words, an appeal for help puts us in the presence of God who loves and acts on our behalf. *We are the adopted children of God* (Gal 4:6).
- Prayer is important. Talk to God in simple words as you would talk to a friend. Of course you are allowed to make requests, but you'll make greater progress in your intimacy with Jesus when you're able to move beyond the *give me this* stage of prayer to a stage of gratitude and listening: *Lord, thank you for this day.*

Reveal to me Your holy will. Teach me to treat all that comes to me throughout the day with peace, with correct thoughts, and with firm conviction that Your will governs all. Amen.

- In faith and trust, we can allow Jesus to envelope us in His goodness, His mercy, and His compassion. We are the objects of His love. His unconditional love is available. All we need is to accept that love and reciprocate by sharing it with others. *People will know that you are My followers, if you love one another.*

- For the physical self He gives us our daily bread. For our soul, the daily bread, *ton epiousion arton*, is a different kind of bread. He gives us what is of essence in life, implying grace and strength at each moment of the day, necessary for our spiritual sustenance.

- In your mind's eye, see yourself as you are today. Hear a voice calling you by name. Recognize the voice as that of Jesus. Turn toward Him and see that He is beckoning to you. As you draw near to Him, He takes you into a gentle embrace. Allow yourself to be still in His embrace. Tell Jesus you want to have a close relationship with Him. This is a request He always grants.

Epilogue

It has been a most rewarding experience to write this book. Above all, it makes me happy that you have been reading it. It is my hope that it will serve as a companion on the road that leads to our Lord and Savior Jesus Christ. It is my personal conviction that the answer to our feelings of abandonment, loneliness, rejection, and despair is to develop an intimacy with Jesus. Focus, commitment, prayer, and determination are needed to sense Jesus in your heart. To paraphrase St. Paul: *With Jesus in me, I can do anything that is good and worthwhile.* In His presence you will find strength, comfort, compassion, joy, and love. In difficult times He is there to provide direction. He does not want you to feel pain and does everything to provide healing.

You are no longer alone. He is with you and loves you dearly, and you are with Him. This can be the time that you wake up in the morning and feel grateful for another day and wonderful about everything around you: the beauty of the sunrise, the glory of nature, the colors of the flowers, the marvel of the mountains, the ecstasy of the ocean, and the thrill of meeting your best friend. With Jesus by your side, you look at life with His eyes, favorably, non-judgmentally, and with love and compassion. When you are critical and judge everything, take an honest look at what you are judging. It could be that something you cannot control is troubling you. Where is Jesus at that moment? Isn't He still standing by you, offering His understanding and love? As you invite him into your heart you will feel happier and healthier, and you will be facing life with all its complexities, challenges, and conflicts without fear or intimidation. *God's perfect love casts out any fear* (1 John 4:18).

Now your task ahead is to continue each day to practice His virtues in serving others through love, forgiving yourself and others for wrongs committed. To serve God is to love God through others; it is to fully realize God's plan for each one of us. This truth has existed for a long time in our hearts, but most of us find it difficult to apply. *Not one of us lives for oneself and no one dies for oneself. For if we live, we live for the Lord, and if we die, we die for the Lord; so then, whether we live or die, we are the Lord's* (Rm 14:7–9). The law of God is fulfilled in one statement: *You shall love your neighbor as yourself* (Gal 5:14). This is the door by which Jesus leads us into intimacy with Himself.

You and I are aware that our love for each other is not unconditional. Only God provides unconditional love. His love helps us live in an unloving world, especially if our own parents never gave us unconditional love. As we mature in our faith, God's love of us is immense, and so is His forgiveness when we admit our sins and repent. Let Jesus inspire our thoughts, our gestures, our behavior, our work, and our relationships with others. In our prayers we can call on His mystical presence to reveal His will to us, to put in our minds the thought that He is a loving God.

In the Gospels, Jesus repeats the sentence: *You are the light of the world* (Mt 5:13–14). That means you and I are the light. If we let the light pass through us, it has the power to eliminate all darkness imaginable. In His presence we are not the light, but He gives us the ability to welcome the light. We are like light bulbs that measure out the light, to give it boundaries, and to make it a reality.

You are the instrument of God's light: you are the light bulb that enlightens your surroundings. *Let your light shine before men that they may see your good deeds and praise your Father in heaven* (Mt 5:16). You need to be conscious of His presence, walking before you, watching your steps, protecting you and uncovering your daily plan. He instills in you the enthusiasm necessary to be at His service each day, so you will be capable of revealing Him to the world. He places the right words in your mouth, so that you will remain His emissary, His ambassador, and His servant. By His wisdom He will correct your thoughts, rectify your actions, and develop capacities for you to concentrate on Him. His light will dispel your doubts, your worries, your hesitations, and it will give you ardor and the eloquence to speak of Him with boldness. He will prepare the path by which you can reach the hearts of others, treating them with dignity, respect, and, when disagreeing with them, doing so courteously.

As I bring this epilogue to a close, I will add the tender words of a man who modeled and spread the teachings of Christ during his earthly life, and who is now enjoying a face-to-face, in-depth relationship with his Master, our Lord Jesus Christ. This was St. Basil of Caesarea, who lived in the fourth century. He said, *The desire of God is not learned by a teaching coming from the outside. From the time we begin to exist, a kind of seed is planted in us; this seed is the interior beginning of Love. We welcome Love by living the Commandments of God. The process of perfection consists in cultivating Love with care within us and nourishing it with intelligence.*

Love brings forth much fruit in us or, to say it in another way, Love is expressed in us through our qualities that are detectable, visible, concrete, simple, and engaging. Remember St. Paul's definition of love. *Love is patient, love is kind. It is not jealous, it is not pompous, it is not inflated, it is not rude, it does not seek its own interests, it is not quick-tempered, it does not brood over injury, it does not rejoice over wrongdoing but rejoices in the truth. It bears all things, believes in all things, endures all things* (1 Cor 13:4–7). This form of Love is God's presence in each of us. It is easy to understand when we read the Epistle to the Hebrews (13:20–21). It is an affirmation that can apply to each one of us. *May the God of peace . . . make you complete in everything that is good so that you will do his will, working within you that which is pleasing in His sight through Jesus Christ. Amen.*

Notes

About the Author

Dr. Peter M. Kalellis is a psychotherapist, marriage and family therapist, lecturer and writer. He has a doctorate in clinical psychology and is the author of many books, including the bestseller *Restoring Relationships: Five Things to Try Before You Say Goodbye* and *Twenty Secrets for Healing Thoughts, Feelings and Relationships*, also available from Crossroad. His practice is located in Westfield, New Jersey.

Tian Dayton, Ph.D.
MOTHER MOTHERING
How to Teach Kids to Say What They Feel and Feel What They Say

From her appearances on *Oprah* to her role as a mother, professor, and counselor, Tian Dayton helps us to see the importance of the mother-child relationship. How do children actually learn to articulate their emotional needs? Dr. Dayton offers a remarkable solution, showing how mothers can guide their children to emotional literacy in order to find their true selves, express creativity, and lead productive lives.

978-0-8245-2340-4, paperback